The E.M.P.O.W.E.R.H.E.R. Blueprint
Empowerment Strategies for Women of Faith on the Rise

Elevated
Minds
Persistently
Overcoming Obstacles
Winning
Every
Realm

Her
Empowerment
Revolution

Chanelle Coleman

For bulk purchases, please contact Chanelle Coleman Wesley at shesaidyestoherself@gmail.com

ISBN: 979-8-9854076-6-2 Print
ISBN: 979-8-9854076-5-5 E-book

All Scripture references are taken from the King James Version of the Bible, unless otherwise indicated.

Dedication

This book is lovingly dedicated to my six amazing children and three precious grandchildren:

Taquan, Tatiyahna, Takari, Tavarius, Tarajah, Julian, Ava, and Amira.

You are my greatest joy and my proudest accomplishment. Each of you has given my life meaning beyond words, and I am forever grateful that God entrusted you to me.

Dream with your eyes wide open, and remember—the only person who can hold you back is you.

May God's grace cover you always, and may Christ remain the love, the life, and the center of your hearts. **My earnest prayer is that we will all wear a crown and be reunited on the sea of glass in the new heavens and new earth at the return of Jesus.**

This book also honors the life and legacy of my beloved daughter, Taniyah Jenee' Lee, who will forever remain my heartbeat.

Niyah—rest in power, my Heartbeat. Until we meet again on resurrection morning, I love you to life.

With all my love,
Mom

Special Acknowledgements

To those who preordered The EmpowerHER Blueprint, I want to extend my deepest gratitude. Your belief in this project has not only been the foundation of its creation, but your support has watered the seeds that turned this vision into reality. You've shown the power of faith and commitment, and because of you, this book is now possible. Thank you for being part of this journey and for empowering the message of transformation and growth. This book belongs to you as much as it does to me. Let's continue to rise, unapologetically and powerfully, together.

Daily Affirmations

I am deserving of success, happiness, and fulfillment. No one can dim my light unless I allow it. I stand firm in my identity and my purpose. I know who I am and whose I am. Daily, I will remind myself that I am capable of achieving greatness. My dreams are valid, and my voice deserves to be heard. I will relentlessly chase my dreams. I will no longer operate in fear.

I vow to be authentic and unapologetic when it comes to loving me. To every closed door and denied opportunity, I'm coming back to get you because I owe me. Every day, I will rise to break glass ceilings. And if I fall, I will get back up, adjust my crown, and relentlessly chase my passions. Fearlessly, I will pursue my dreams, my goals, and every aspiration. My God is on my side. I will not fail.

Personal Declaration

I, _____, declare my commitment to breaking barriers and uplifting those around me. I will unapologetically wear my crown, fully embracing my identity as a leader. My worth is inherent, undeniable, and I will walk in it fiercely, with boldness.

2. I will carry myself with grace and confidence, knowing I am deserving of success.

3. I will rise above the challenges life presents to me, understanding that every "no" brings me closer to my "yes." Failure isn't a delay in receiving the desired result—it's never trying at all.

4. I will embrace my destiny with open arms, taking bold steps toward my goals. I affirm that I am capable of creating the life I desire. God is on my side, and I will not fail.

5. My God is my protector, my provider, my rock, and my shield—therefore, no weapon formed against me shall prosper. I AM More Than A Conqueror.

Sis, this book is your invitation to plant and water seeds sown in seasons of waiting, discouragement, sorrow, grief, joy, peace, prosperity, and resilience. Life will continue to present you with both blessings and challenges — yet, despite it all, God has called you to bloom unapologetically, wherever you find yourself in life.

My Bold Invitation for You

In this book, I'm sharing 19 powerful strategies that, if you apply them, will move you from waiting on it to walking in it. At the end, I'll issue a bold call to action for those who are ready to take decisive steps toward their purpose. I want to see you walking boldly into your divinely designed purpose.

I'll also invite you to join our empowering community, attend life-changing classes, receive personalized coaching, and engage in virtual/live events to support your journey. Why? Because you owe you.

Are you ready? Let's go!

Chapter One

There's No Elevator to the Top—You've Got to Take the Stairs

CONSISTENCY *Hello Gorgeous*....

Affirmation:

No Investment—No Reward

Transparency moment: I've had many intended destinations, but whether I reached them or not depended heavily on the mode of travel. Sis, let me be clear: if I'm given the choice between a difficult path and a sweat-free route, I'll choose the easy one.

Elevators are my preferred way to travel. Escalators? Not so much— I still carry some childhood anxiety—but hey, don't judge me. Stairs? Forget about it. I'd question how much I really wanted what was on the other side.

The Power of Persistence
There's no elevator to the top; if you want to reach the next level, you've got to take the stairs. We all want success, but

achieving it depends on the actions we take—or refuse to take. Your goals demand sweat, commitment, and sometimes discomfort. If reaching it doesn't stretch you, can it really be the top. Your greatest rewards demand sacrifice.

After losing my daughter, Taniyah, I threw myself into a rigorous workout routine to combat depression. I loved the treadmill, the bike, and other machines—but the stairs? Torture. They demanded persistence, endurance, and pushing past discomfort. And I avoided them whenever I could.

Facing Fear and Choosing Growth

But it wasn't just in the gym, I treated my goals the same way, running from anything that required real sacrifice and calling it self-preservation instead of self sabotage. It's easier to believe a lie rather than to accept an uncomfortable truth. We fear failure, but often, it's our own success that terrifies us. We settle for comfort, avoiding challenges due to perceived risks.

Goals that require commitment can feel uncomfortable, even scary. Fear of failure, fear of success, fear of the unknown—these can make us choose comfort over growth. I've been there. I've avoided the hard path because I thought it required too much.

Have you downplayed your ability to pursue your calling because success would mean stepping outside of your comfort zone? There was a time when I refused to pursue my dreams, paralyzed by the investment I knew I would have to make. We tend to become comfortable in limiting situations, forgetting that our greatest potential demands not just walking or running but flying and soaring. Can you relate?

Rocky: A Lesson in Determination

I know I'm about to date myself with this movie, but here it goes. Rocky, starring Sylvester Stallone, was one of my all-time favorite childhood films. If you haven't seen it, imagine your favorite sport's montage—that was Rocky. One of cinema's most iconic scenes is his stair run. His early attempts were clumsy, but he persisted, dedicating himself to perfecting the skill. With the theme music blaring, he conquers those infamous stairs, each step a testament to his determination, resilience, and relentless consistency.

Climbing with Purpose: Every Step Counts

As a child, this scene taught me that stair workouts build a different kind of muscle, consistency pays off over time, and goals of this magnitude require commitment (and yes, a theme song). Sacrifice isn't linear; it has peaks and valleys, and each stage demands greater investment.

Just like those stairs became my proving ground, faith has its own steps. Every step gives us invaluable lessons on commitment, persistence, and the level of sacrifice required.

Faith and Sacrifice: Lessons from the Mosaic Law

The Mosaic Law illustrates varying degrees of sacrifice through its sacrificial system. Sacrifices served multiple purposes: reconciliation, thankfulness, dedication, or purification. They facilitated worship, atoned for sins, and expressed devotion and gratitude. Some offerings required only portions of the animal to be eaten, sacrificed, or discarded. But burnt offerings were different; they demanded that the entire sacrifice be consumed in the flames.

In life, there are goals that will ask you to place pieces of yourself on the altar. But make no mistake, there will undoubtedly be times when you will be asked to put it all on the altar.

Let's face it. Without complete surrender, there are some levels that can't be accessed. Here's an uncomfortable truth: We desire the unmerited favor of God, but we resist His yoke. We want the overflow with no investment. Everybody wants the blessings and favor of Abraham, but nobody wants to put their "Isaac" on the altar to get it.

Embrace the Climb: Transforming Obstacles into Opportunities
In the pursuit of our dreams, we must be willing to lay it all on the line. No sacrifice, no reward. It's the investment of blood, sweat, and tears that makes the triumph truly worthwhile.

Don't believe me? Skip the elevator—take the stairs. Feel the burn, the fatigue, the resistance. The easy route dulls your anticipation, while the climb tests your commitment. On this journey, expect hills, valleys, mountaintops, plains, and yes—stairs—each demanding your effort and teaching invaluable lessons.

Challenges aren't obstacles; they're your teachers. They equip you with the skills, the endurance, and the insights necessary for personal and spiritual growth. Embrace the stairs—they are not just part of the process—they are the process. The climb isn't easy, but the view from the top? Unquestionably worth it.

Self-Work Activity

---◆---

Let's put what we've learned into action.

Join the She Said Yes to Herself
Unapologetically Stair Challenge.

You've got mountains to climb. So let's
commit to taking the stairs.
For 7 days, commit to taking the stairs to
build discipline, consistency, and the
mindset to embrace the harder path that
leads to greater rewards. It doesn't matter
how many — what matters is consistency.
The more you do it, the easier it will become.
Share your experience on social media using
the hashtags

#SheSaidYesStairChallenge #womenoffaith.
#empoweredwomenempowerwomen

Chapter Two

Do It Scared

Hello Gorgeous....

Affirmation:

Fear doesn't get to dictate my next move. I do.

Fear No Longer Has Dominion Over Us
Do it scared, Sis. It's your time. It's your turn. It's your season. Do it with your heart trembling, chest pounding, knees knocking, mind racing, palms sweating, stomach twisting, and turning. Do it when your fears threaten to silence your dreams. Do it scared!

When people see me making big moves, they assume that it's because I'm fearless. But that couldn't be further from the truth. Sis, I'm scared, but my fears no longer have permission to stop me from pursuing my dreams. I acknowledge my fear, and turn that nervous energy into momentum.

Instead of asking myself, "Why would I do XYZ?" I ask, "What's on the other side of my fears?" I use that adrenaline as fuel to push past my perceived limitations. I challenge myself to step outside of my comfort zone. I don't wait for my fears to disappear. I move with intention and as I take action my fears begin to fade.

Scared But Unstoppable: The Other Side of Fear

There was a time when the words "I'm scared" gave me permission to abandon my dreams. Fear can sentence us to a life trapped inside a box of limiting beliefs. Have you ever been so consumed with your fears that you couldn't step into your calling?

Most fears are based upon myths — things we imagine will happen. But how many of those fears actually have the probability of coming true? If we did a facts-over-fears analysis, we'd quickly realize that most of our fears are unrealistic and that the pros almost always outweigh the cons.

Scared But Unstoppable: Testing the Edge

Growing up, being able to jump double Dutch rope was a status symbol. I was too afraid of getting hit with the ropes, lacking the ability, or looking silly to participate, so I lived life on the sidelines. I was saddled with my insecurities, too afraid to take action or get into the game. My sister, Salina, was the complete opposite. She didn't just jump rope—she could pick it up, drop it, twist it, turn it, pop, and lock it. I'd watch her mesmerized in amazement.

Eventually, I learned how to turn rope. This was me testing the edge without falling over, so I stuck to turning rope. Unaware of my internal dialogue and mindset, the girls would say, "It's your turn, Chanelle." But I'd just shrug my shoulders and say, "No, that's okay. You go. It's your turn. I'm an all-time turner." And so, I just kept turning rope.

That wasn't the only time fear kept me on the sidelines.

The Eagle: Confronting Fear Head-On

In She Said Yes to Herself Unapologetically, I shared my fear of riding the Eagle — a 127 ft. wooden dual racing roller coaster located at Six Flags Great America in Gurnee, Illinois. I vividly recounted my first experience: waiting in the long line, stomach churning, heart pounding, knees trembling, and hands sweating.

As I inched closer to the top, anxiety set in. I felt the flutter of the butterflies flying in the pit of my stomach. But those butterflies soon turned into grasshoppers, which morphed into gophers, and before long, the gophers transformed into rabbits. I looked in horror at its immense size with all the twists and turns a familiar voice within me whispered, "Chanelle, what are you doing? You aren't supposed to be here."

After all of the waiting and back-and-forth inner dialogue, I don't know how I did it but I finally reached the top. But as I stood at the front of the line, my negative self-talk kicked in.

Mmm!" she said, sucking her teeth and mumbling under her breath. Then came the side-eye. "Girl, you're a fool if you think we're getting on this ride."
It didn't take her long to talk me out of my spot. Fear won, and I took the embarrassing walk of shame back through the crowd.

I offered polite 'excuse me's' while maneuvering through the line headed in the wrong direction. I knew what they were thinking: "She couldn't do it. She couldn't ride the Eagle." But as I walked away, another voice inside me said, "Chanelle, you can do this, and you're not leaving here until you do."

My second attempt at riding the Eagle was even harder than the first. My inner critic taunted me relentlessly: "If you couldn't do it the first time, what makes you think you'll be able to do it this time?" And as I stubbornly inched closer and closer to the top she screamed, "You aren't supposed to be here!"

But this time, I was determined. I silenced my doubts with one firm declaration as I got closer to the top. "You're not leaving this park until you do!"

With no roller coaster experience, I sat in the first car. I didn't know it then, but—big mistake! As I entered the bucket seat, my body felt weak. I desperately searched for a seatbelt that wasn't there. As the ride prepared to take off, the attendant began to give instructions. His commands sounded a lot like Charlie Brown's Teacher, "Wah, wah, wah, wah, wah, wah, wah, wah, wah, wah." My heart pounded in my ears, as I gripped the bar, dug my feet into the floorboard, and tried to calm my nerves.

The ride started deceptively smooth, and for a moment, I thought I had overreacted. But as we slowly made the steep ascent, panic crept in. I watched in horror as the park attendees, and rides grew smaller as we made our way to the top. When we reached our highest height, we hung suspended in the air for a moment, I held my breath. I think they purposely let you hang just to make you question why you got on the ride. Meanwhile, my inner critic was too busy shaking her head to say anything.

I've always been a person of faith even as a child. My mother had taught me to call upon the name of the Lord whenever I was in trouble. So I did what any sensible being in this situation would do — I closed my eyes and I began to pray. "Lord, if you get me off of this thing I promise -" and before I could finish my prayer we began plunging 147 feet.

I squeezed the bar tightly, pressing my feet into the floorboard as we twisted and turned. Around me, people were laughing. I opened my eyes, looked over, and saw their happy faces glowing with excitement, and I wondered why I wasn't having fun. Then it hit me: maybe I wasn't enjoying myself because my hands weren't raised. I considered putting my hands up, but my inner critic found her voice and snapped: "Fool, don't you dare!"

Ignoring her, I nervously raised my arms and tried to relax. That was all well and good—until the next drop. My inner voice screamed, "Girl, if you don't put your hands down and hold on!" I looked at the approaching drop and enthusiastically agreed. When the ride finally ended, I was ecstatic. I did it!

Living Beyond Fear: The Power of Action

The rush of adrenaline was unreal. I had finally conquered the unthinkable! I went on to ride the Eagle several more times before I left the park that day. This experience helped me ride other coasters. As I faced various roller coasters, that inner voice didn't go away; however, each time I confronted my fears, the voice grew a little softer until I could barely hear her trying to convince me to get off the rides. To this day, no matter how many times I've visited that amusement park, I never leave without riding the Eagle.

This experience has taught me to live my life beyond fear. I recognize that there will be steps I need to take action on. And now, as I embrace an empowered lifestyle, I dream with my eyes wide open. I seek that familiar feeling I experienced the first time I rode the Eagle.

Am I fearful when I take decisive actions? Yes, I'm scared—but I refuse to let fear dictate my actions. I understand that nervousness is part of the process. Instead of running from it, I lean into it and use that energy to push forward. I use this feeling as a temperature check to know when I'm playing small. If my dreams don't stir up that familiar feeling, I know I'm not dreaming big enough. And Sis, the same is true for you!

Self-Work Activity

◆

Each time I take a leap of faith, I'm rewarded.
As a result, I become less fearful and gain
more confidence in taking the next steps.
Let's talk about your fears.

What's getting in the way of realizing your
dreams, and why?
What's waiting on the other side of those
fears?
How much longer can you afford to stay
stuck, immobilized by fear?

Journal about your dreams. Describe what it
would feel like to accomplish your goals.

Are you ready to recommit to realizing your
dreams? It's time for YOU to get to work! We
have mountains to climb. Start climbing, and
I'll see you on the other side!

Chapter Three

Push, Sis! It's in You.

Hello Gorgeous.....

Affirmation:

Everything you want is on the other side of fear—go get it.

From Pressure to Power: Birthing Purpose Through Pain
I'm excited to serve women on their journey toward hope, healing, and empowerment. Why? Because I know what it feels like to hit rock bottom. I remember the days when I wasn't living my dreams because I was too busy living my fears.

Too often, we dim our own light because we're too scared to shine. We question our calling, our abilities, and even God's timing. We run from purpose or struggle to discover it. We chase validation, battle limiting beliefs, and replay past mistakes, all while holding onto a flicker of hope that our dreams are still possible.

That conviction that whispers to us, reminding us that there's more, compels us to keep moving forward. But let's be real: if it were easy, we'd all be living the dream. So why aren't we living it? Do you want the truth? Most of us are stuck somewhere between being too scared to dream and

waiting for our goals to materialize. We want the prize, but we shrink back from the process, because the process involves pain.

Why Your Breakthrough Demands a Push

In the pursuit of our ideal life, we're all somewhere between infertility, pregnancy, labor, delivery, or helping our dreams grow up. This journey demands pain, patience, and positioning. In this chapter, I'll use labor and delivery as a metaphor for every unrealized dream.

In my first book in this series, *She Said Yes to Herself Unapologetically: The Empowerment Guide for Women*, I explored the delicate interplay between pain and progress.

Let's use three key insights from this book to explain this dynamic:

Point #1: Your Pain is Parallel to Your Progress. Wherever pain is present, progress is within reach.

Point #2: Transition Never Happens in a Comfortable Place. True growth requires a shift—in posture, placement, mindset, and attitude. Change happens outside comfort zones, beyond limiting beliefs, and past perceived limitations.

Point #3: The Power is in Your Perception. What you believe shapes your words, thoughts, and actions, ultimately influencing who you become and what you can achieve.

The Process Hurts, but the Promise is Worth It

Too often, fear of pain, failure, or even success paralyzes us, keeping us stuck in what feels safe and familiar. But what if you committed to keep pursuing your dreams until you saw the outcome you desired?

How would your life transform if your lifestyle demonstrated that you were in heavy expectation of receiving countless miracles? Imagine overcoming your perceived limitations, silencing excuses, and achieving your greatest wins. How different would your life be if your dreams shifted from possibilities to nonnegotiable realities?

Your Moment of Breakthrough
Let's unpack our acronym P.U.S.H.

· **P. Perseverance is Developed Under Pressure.**
Relentless pursuits produce unimaginable victories. Walking into your greatest season will lead you to go through the fire in order to get it.
· **U. Unshakable Faith Moves Beyond Comfort Zones.**
Radical faith will elicit radical moves.
· **S. Setbacks are Opportunities for Set-Ups.** *Oftentimes, we see opposition as an indicator to check out of our dreams and realign with our fears. But setbacks provide the added benefits of knowledge, experience, and insight that can position you to realize your greatest wins.*
· **H. Healed or Hostage You Choose.** *We don't get to choose the storms life presents to us, but how we emerge from them is entirely up to us.*

Today, I'm a bestselling author, international speaker, coach, publisher, founder, and editor-in-chief of Hustl' HER Magazine. I build platforms, host events, and create opportunities for authors, speakers, and coaches to inspire women across the globe. But I didn't start here—my journey was birthed out of pain, loss, and the decision to keep pushing when giving up felt easier.

After the death of my daughter Taniyah, I entered a season where all I saw was the abyss—darkness surrounded me on every side. I had given up my will to live, convinced my surviving children would be better off without me. I teetered on the edge of life's cliff, willing myself to jump.

Then I heard my daughter Tatiyahna's words: "Mama, we need you! Mama, we need you! Mama, we need you too!" In that moment, something inside me shifted. Her words didn't just reach me, they pulled me back, reminded me of purpose, and gave me the strength to step away from the edge. Something deep inside whispered, "Push Sis, It's in You!"

Harnessing the Power Within
And just like me, you have your own mountains to climb. Life has knocked you down, but you made the decision to get back up. And despite what you've been through, you're still standing. Even in our darkest moments, we are never alone. God is with us. He has promised to never leave us or forsake us. And if God is standing for us, who or what can be against us?

Maybe you're wondering is pain a part of the process. Yes. Pain is a necessary agitator. Without it, we'd stay complacent. It helps us recognize purpose, measure progress, sharpen focus, and positions us for breakthrough.

I had to push past my pain to experience progress, and the same is true for you. Through the pages of this book I'll walk with you and together, we can emerge on the other side of the valley. And we don't have to look like what we've been through— 5 seconds, 5 minutes, 5 days, 5 weeks, 5 months, or 5 years ago. Your breakthrough is waiting on the other side of your pain!

Things are no different in the labor and delivery room. Pain and progress coexist in the same space at the same time.

But we can't access one without navigating through the other. Without the benefit of physicians, doulas, or specialty teams and equipment many would-be mothers and babies would not survive!

Visualize an expectant mother on her delivery bed. She is worn out, exhausted, and desperate for her breakthrough. She's ready to bring her baby into the world, but she can't push before her body is fully positioned to deliver. Her face is drenched in sweat, her body is racked with pain, but when the baby is finally in position, and she's fully dilated, the physician or doula will signal the moment to push!

Redefining What's Possible

Today, many of us are in the same position. You may or may not be expecting a baby, but you're birthing dreams, goals, and ideas. You're pregnant with purpose and possibilities that will produce businesses, podcasts, movements, platforms, degrees, and more. Without the right strategist or coach, these dreams can become haunting nightmares.

In this season, you need guidance, someone who has walked through pain and now sits at a different vantage point. Someone who provides experience, strategies, and perspective. Without the right support our dreams could stall. I've been there, and I want to walk this part of the journey with you.

Let me help you, Sis! It's time to get off the sidelines and get into the game. You might be asking, "Chanelle, when is it going to be my turn?" You may be waiting for a sign before giving yourself permission to move. Sis, this is it. This is your moment. It's your time, it's your turn, it's your season. Now is the time to push.

Push! It's in you! Push—it's in you! Push, Sis—it's in you!

Self-Work Activity

◆

Push, Sis—It's In You: 10 Bold Questions to Uncover Your Weights & Blind Spots

1. What limiting beliefs have I been holding onto that don't serve me?
· Identify the thoughts that have been keeping you stuck. Which ones need to be discarded for you to move forward?

2. Where in my life am I playing small or shrinking myself so I can feel comfortable?
· Reflect on the moments where you've held back your true potential to fit in or avoid conflict. How can you step into your full power today?

3. What fear or doubt keeps resurfacing, and how does it limit my decisions?
· Dive deep into your fears. What decisions have you avoided because of them, and how can you begin to face them head-on?

4. What unresolved pain or trauma am I carrying, and how is it affecting my present?
· Acknowledge the past pain you might still be carrying. How is it affecting your actions, relationships, and future aspirations?

5. What negative patterns or cycles do I repeatedly find myself in, and why do I keep returning to them?
· Identify recurring negative behaviors or situations. What needs to shift for you to break the cycle and create new habits?

Chapter Four

Speak to the Storm

Hello Gorgeous....

Empowering Declaration:

Sis, repeat after me:

God is the head of my life. He told me to speak to the every situation and circumstance that attempts to rise up against me.

*I declare His authority over my life.
I embrace my power to speak life into every storm that seeks to overwhelm me. With unwavering faith, I command fear, doubt, and negativity to cease.*

I stand firm in my identity and purpose, knowing that God has equipped me to weather any challenge.

I will not be defined by my storms; instead, I will be defined by how I rise above them, transforming adversity into strength.

Today, I speak audacious courage, unflinching hope, and victory over my circumstances, and I choose to walk boldly in my divine purpose.

Speaking to the Impossible

Most of us would agree that inanimate objects lack feelings, reasoning abilities, and the power to perform tasks. Countless times, I've wished my house would clean itself—but it never has. I think we've all felt this frustration. And let me be clear: if, for some strange reason, my house obeyed my command, it would be my last day in that house. In the Word of God, we see moments when His people were commanded to speak to inanimate objects—things that could not respond:

- *Moses and Aaron spoke to a rock, and water flowed.*

- *Joshua spoke to the sun, and it stood still, giving Israel a decisive victory in battle.*

- *Elijah spoke to the heavens, and fire fell, consuming his enemies.*

- *King Hezekiah requested a sign, and the sundial moved backward to affirm the prophet's words.*

And at the words of Jesus Christ, storms ceased, the dead were raised, sickness fled, and demonic forces fell.

These victories were obtained through the power of words. Scripture commands us to speak to mountains, sickness, death, and every weapon of the enemy, knowing they must submit to the powerful name of Jesus Christ.

Proverbs 18:21 reminds us: "Death and life are in the power of the tongue, and those that love it will eat the fruit of it." Both visible and invisible matter responds to words. Provocative, isn't it?

Claiming Victory Over Life's Storms

Words carry weight—they can build or destroy, give life or bring death. God demonstrates this most clearly in creation: the world came into being and continues to exist by His words. When He speaks, the supernatural unfolds; heaven and earth respond, producing His intended outcome.

We might think it makes sense to speak to obstacles only when the odds are favorable—but God calls us to speak when obstacles feel insurmountable. These barriers are opportunities to strengthen our faith. Sis speak boldly, daringly, and without apology—whether you're confronting giants, turbulent seas, or mountains.

Trials as a Divine Classroom

I've faced many storms, but none shaped my ability to speak to obstacles like Taniyah's medical challenges. Her multi-complex health conditions were my storm. I learned that trials produce one of two things: faith or doubt. The storm wasn't sent to break me. It was sent to make me. What looked like devastation became a divine classroom, where God taught me to trust beyond what I could see. The visible is temporary; the invisible is eternal.

Bold Declarations for Uncertain Times

There were moments when Taniyah's life hung between life and death. I spoke life while everything around me screamed death. I grieved silently, managing a state I call happy-hurt, mourning missed milestones while believing they were deferred, not denied. I chronicled many of these moments in my first book, *Naked & Not Ashamed: The Transformational Devotional Experience.*

After two anoxic brain injuries, her prognosis was grim. Doctors urged me to remove her from life support. Every earthly measure said one thing: death. But I knew that God, and God alone has the final say. I trusted in the sovereignty of my God. He can do whatever He wants to, when He wants to, how He wants to. He is GOD. My faith said, "Let God be true, and every dismal prognosis a liar."

I trusted Him to do exceedingly and abundantly above all I could ask, think, or imagine.

While specialists wrote her off, I gave thanks for what God was ready to do. I read Scripture over and over to Taniyah, rehearsed His promises in prayer, trusting He was able and willing to protect this treasure He had given me. I watched her cling to life support, become a regular resident in ICUs and trauma rooms, lie motionless for 7–8 months, yet still follow small commands, sip her favorite chocolate shake, laugh, and defy the odds. Most importantly, she smiled—something I was told I would never see.

Taniyah came into this world a fighter and went out as one. Born a 28-week preemie weighing 2 pounds, 4 ounces, God extended her life repeatedly. A chronic asthmatic with recurring bouts with RSV, Respiratory Syncytial Virus. God's mercy continued to lengthen her days. I was blessed with 16 years with this wondrously amazing being because I learned to speak to my storms.

Rising Above the Waves of Struggle

Life puts us either into, out of, or right in the middle of a storm. So, what's your storm? Maybe it doesn't look like mine, but we all have challenges that shake us to our core. I'm here to tell you—speak to your circumstances. Declare and decree victory. Believe God for the outcome. These spiritual battles are training grounds, teaching us to depend fully on Him.

When the storms of life rage around us, it's easy to get lost in the crashing waves, the howling winds, and the dark, threatening skies. But remember this: the Master of the Seas is with you, just as He was with the disciples back then—no matter where you are in your storm.

It might feel exactly like it did for them—you're in the ship of life, Jesus is there, but He seems asleep. The winds roar. The waves batter you from all sides. Water pours in, and hope seems gone. Like the disciples, you cry out, "Lord, carest Thou not that we perish?" (Mark 4:38). But just as He did then, He rises, He speaks, and the storm obeys. "Peace, be still." (Mark 4:39).

Maybe your storm looks like walking on water. The seas are rough, the winds blow, and doubt whispers: "Why did He call you here?" You start to sink, overwhelmed. And in that moment, with waves crashing over you, you cry out:
"Master, save me!"

And He does. Immediately. Christ reaches into the depths, lifts you up, and helps you stand on the turbulent waters. He looks you in the eyes and asks the question that pierces your soul: "Oh ye of little faith, why do you doubt?" (Matthew 14:31).

Sis, don't trust only what you see. Speak to your storm. Declare it gone. Stand in faith and boldly say, "Peace, be still." The storm may rage—but you will rise above it, stronger, wiser, and victorious.

Self-Work Activity

◆

Journaling Your Storm: A Faith-Driven Self-Work Activity
It's your time to step into your power and face the storms in your life. This activity is all about reflection, declaration, and action—transforming fear into faith, doubt into courage, and obstacles into opportunities.

Step 1: Identify Your Storm
Take a moment to pause and reflect. What's the storm you are facing right now? It could be a challenge at work, a relationship struggle, a health concern, or a fear holding you back. Write it down in your journal. Be honest, be raw, and name it clearly.
Prompt:
"The storm I am facing is..."

Step 2: Speak to Your Storm
Remember, Scripture shows us the power of speaking to mountains, seas, and circumstances. You have that same authority through Christ. Declare your faith over the storm. Use bold, powerful words—write them down.
Prompt:
"I speak to my storm and command it to... because God has said..."

Step 3: Reflect on Your Faith
Think about a time you faced a challenge and overcame it. What did you learn about your resilience, your faith, or your strength? How can those lessons guide you now?
Prompt:
"I have overcome before, and I will overcome again by..."

Self-Work Activity

Step 4: Plan Your Next Steps
Transformation requires action. What can you do today—or this week—to move through your storm with courage and intention? Write down one to three actionable steps.
Prompt:
"To navigate this storm, I will..."

Step 5: Optional Sharing for Community
If you feel led, share a short reflection, excerpt, or declaration from your journaling on social media. Inspire others by showing that facing storms with faith is possible.
Tag me @Chanelle Coleman Wesley and use:
#JournalingYourStorm #SheSaidYesToHerself
#EmpoweredWomenEmpower

Instagram: Chanelle Coleman Wesley
LinkedIn: Chanelle Coleman Wesley
Tik Tok: Chanelle Coleman Wesley
Facebook: Chanelle Coleman Wesley

Chapter Five

Don't look back Sis—You Don't Live There Anymore

Hello Gorgeous.....

Scripture:

Like a dog returns to its vomit, so is the fool who repeats his foolishness. Proverbs 26:11

It's impossible to look in two directions at once. Active seeing requires your full attention on the object in front of you, forcing you to abandon distractions. The human eye, part of the sensory nervous system, does more than just see: it reacts to light, processes visual information, helps maintain balance, and even regulates our circadian rhythm. But beyond its physical functions, the eye is a window to the soul, granting access to the heart and mind.

This is why the Scripture says, "by beholding we become changed." Jesus' words, "Remember Lot's Wife!" (Luke 17:32), serves as a stark warning about the danger of turning back.

Your Power Lies Ahead Not Behind

Genesis 19 details the chain of events that led to the destruction of two of the most infamous cities in history: Sodom and Gomorrah. Scripture tells us that Lot pitched his tent toward Sodom—a city where every evil imagination was indulged, standing in sharp contrast to the life he and his family once shared with faithful Abraham (Genesis 13:12). Yet as Lot watched the city day after day, his perception began to shift. The next time the Bible mentions him, we find Lot and his family firmly trapped within the city's grasp.

The city's occupants were unknowingly standing in judgment before God, oblivious to the pending sentence that loomed over them. In a final act of mercy, God sent two angels, appearing as men, to witness before heaven and the world whether the people's sins warranted devastating judgment.

Seeing the strangers in the middle of the city square, Lot wanted to be hospitable, but he also knew the two men alone in the heart of the city would be easy prey. He welcomed them into the safety of his home for the evening, then urged them to continue their travels at daybreak.

He presumed they were safe behind doors— until a crowd of men descended upon the house. The mob, composed of both young and old men, surrounded the house, threatening to assault Lot if he did not hand over his guests. Their intent was clear: they wanted to rape the men. In response, the angels struck the men with blindness, rescuing Lot. Yet even in their blindness they continued to search in vain for an opening into the house (Genesis 19:1-11). **Pg. 26**

The impending destruction of the twin cities, which would take their inhabitants and the world by overwhelming surprise, forced the family to make life-or-death decisions if they desired to be spared. On that fateful night, an awesome message was delivered: "Leave this place at once. Tonight, these cities will be destroyed." And although the angels pronounced its impending doom, Lot and his family remained nestled within the city's walls (Genesis 19:13-15).

No Growth In the Shadows of Yesterday
It wasn't until Lot, his two daughters, and his wife were escorted out of the city, hand in hand, by these heavenly beings that the family was finally propelled into action. As they made their way out, the last warning was given, "Flee into the mountains. Don't Look Back." As the family ran for their lives from the looming destruction, with calamity nipping at their heels, a burning desire for what was beamed in the heart of Lot's wife. She was leaving her remaining children, friends, possessions, and the life she had come to know to venture into the unknown. And although they were poised to escape, the town and its rotting influence had made a lasting impression on all of them.

While running for her life, her mind romanticized her time in that wretched city and she obeyed the deadly urge to have one last look. One look was all it took! As she turned around to look at her beloved city she was instantly transformed into a pillar of salt (Genesis 19:26).

That brief moment in scripture embodies her as the bodily representation of looking back. The residue of a place doesn't disappear just because you leave it behind. What Sodom had planted still showed up in Lot and his family.

While the three survivors managed to escape the destruction of Sodom and Gomorrah, Lot's willingness to offer his daughters the mob, his choice to remain in the

city after the warning, and their subsequent drunken and incestuous behavior reveal that the influence of these cities had not fully left them.

Your Power Lies Ahead and Not Behind
We can't talk about transformation without addressing the power of letting go. Lot's wife is a stark reminder. God had already pulled her out of destruction, but her longing for what was behind cost her her future. One look back turned her into a pillar of salt. Jesus Himself warned in
Luke 17:32: "Remember Lot's wife."
Why? Because the temptation to look back is strong — even when God is calling us forward.

And I know that temptation all too well. There was a time that I operated this way, trying to walk back down memory lane with people, places, and things, even though I knew they no longer served me. We have a tendency to attempt to relive, revisit, or revive dead connections believing that somehow things will be different, or that we can take one last look and walk away unscathed. But looking back to revisit places we've already been prevents forward progress and momentum.

Most times we didn't leave these spaces willingly. No, we were forced out, we were pushed out, and just like Lot and his family, we were running for our lives. It was pain, tragedy, and heartache that drove us to our knees to plead with God for deliverance. But once we were freed, something within us desired to take one last look. How many of you can relate?

Proverbs 26:11 illustrates the idea that foolish behavior often tends to repeat itself, much like a dog returning to it's vomit. This analogy chronicles the journey of a dog

Proverbs 26:11 illustrates the idea that foolish behavior often tends to repeat itself, much like a dog returning to it's vomit. This analogy chronicles the journey of a dog returning to something unpleasant, an experience it has already expelled from its body.

A fool repeats actions or behaviors that are harmful or unwise, despite knowing the consequences. It suggests that despite experiencing negative outcomes or consequences from their actions, fools are unable or unwilling to learn from their previous mistakes and continue to engage in foolish behavior. It serves as a cautionary warning against repeating past mistakes and encourages individuals to learn from their experiences and make wiser choices.

That's not just Bible — that's life. We've all been there.

How many times has looking back prompted you to play the fool? The definition of insanity is doing the same thing but expecting a different result. It would be inconceivable to watch a dog revisit its vomit, yet we do the same thing when we attempt to re-engage with people or circumstances we were forced to disconnect from. Most likely, the reason the relationship failed will be the instigator in helping to dissolve the mended connection.

I had to learn that people, places, and things are not permitted to access me through a revolving door. I refuse to

place myself back into places that I had to pray my way out of. That missed call was a blessing. The person coming into a room you exited 5 minutes ago is a byproduct of unmerited favor.

Letting Go of What No Longer Serves You

Our last insight is the psychological aspect behind this proverb. It highlights the concept of habituation, denoting the fact that over time we become desensitized to negative consequences. Despite our initial aversion, pain, or discomfort, repeated exposure to certain behaviors can diminish our perceived severity, making it easier for us to rationalize or justify engaging in them again. Understanding this psychological phenomenon sheds light on why we sometimes willfully continue to continue to repeat mistakes despite knowing better.

Sis, let me remind you: your power isn't behind you, it's ahead of you. Don't turn back, don't take one last look — what God has for you is too good to miss.

Self-Work Activity

◆

Release & Renewal: Don't Return to the Vomit —
Paper Burning Nature Walk

Here's what we've learned: our power lies ahead, not behind.
Looking back keeps us tied to cycles that sabotage us.

Psychology calls it habituation — the brain's tendency to
crave what feels familiar, even if it's destructive. But faith
calls us to break free.

*To truly embrace this freedom, we must take intentional action.
Think of the habits, relationships, or mindsets you've already
"expelled" from your life—the things you know no longer serve
you. Proverbs 26:11 calls them out plainly: "Like a dog returns to
its vomit, so is the fool who repeats his foolishness." This activity
will help you release the past, confront the temptation to return,
and step boldly into what God has for you next.*

This combined exercise merges the cleansing power of nature
with the symbolic act of burning, allowing you to release what
no longer serves you and step into a new chapter.

Step #1 – Preparation
Before your walk, write down anything you feel you need to
release: habits, relationships, mindsets, or patterns that
you've been tempted to return to—your "vomit" moments.
Be honest and specific.

Step #2 – Nature Walk
Head out on a walk in a nearby park, trail, or even your
backyard. With every step, reflect on your "vomit" moments:
- **What have I been tempted to return to?**

Self-Work Activity

- How has returning held me back from the life God has for me?

Breathe deeply and notice the natural surroundings—the trees, birds, breeze, and earth beneath your feet. Let these cycles of nature remind you that life moves forward, not backward.

Step #3 – Reflective Walking
Observe the constant cycles of growth in nature—leaves falling, streams flowing, seasons changing. Let this remind you that, like nature, you are always evolving. Each step is a chance to release what's behind and embrace what's ahead.

Step #4 – Finding Your Spot & Burning
Find a safe, controlled place to burn your papers (firepit, grill, campfire, or a portable fire starter in a non-flammable dish). One by one, read each item aloud and release it: **"I release this [name your vomit moment]. I will not return to it. I choose forward momentum and God's purpose for my life."**

Step #5 – Affirmation of Release
As the flames consume the papers, speak aloud: **"I release the past, and with it, all that no longer serves me. I refuse to return to the vomit. I choose peace, freedom, and the limitless possibilities ahead."**

Step #6 – Silent Reflection
Spend a few minutes in silence, reflecting on what you've released:

Self-Work Activity

- What would my life look like if I never returned to this "vomit" again?
- How will releasing this create space for God's blessings and growth?

Step #7 – Walk Forward with Intention
Continue your walk, feeling the weight lift with each step. Step into your future intentionally, knowing your power lies ahead, not in the past.

Reflection Questions
- What "vomit" have you been tempted to return to in your life?
- What patterns, people, or situations have drained you that you need to release?
- If God has already delivered you, why would you consider returning?

Declaration
"I will not look back. My power lies ahead, and I refuse to go back to anything God had to rescue me from."

Chapter Six

Prophecies in the Bag: What You Believe You Become

Hello Gorgeous.....

Scripture:

"As a man thinketh so is he..." Proverbs 23:7 (first part).

The Choice Between Empowerment and Limitation
In a city not too far from your own, lived an old bag woman, revered by the townsfolk for her fortune-telling. She was more than what she appeared, an enigma shrouded in mystery. People traveled from near and far to hear her predictions. Her tales captivated listeners, and her words seemed to hold a power all their own. Remarkably, it seemed her predictions always came true.

One day, two young girls from the same side of town went to visit the old bag woman, eager to know what the future held for them. Both were filled with excitement and anticipation as they walked the two miles to reach her home. Upon entering they found the scene exactly as they imagined: the older woman sat quietly in her rocking chair, staring at them. "I've been expecting you," she said.

The floor creaked beneath the old rocking chair as the woman began to hum. "What will we be--" one girl started to ask, but the old woman cut her off. "Shhh!" Suddenly, she rose and moved toward the kettle stove. From her pocket, she pulled three mint leaves, dropped them into the boiling water, and stirred with an old wooden spoon. Her gaze locked onto the girls as she began her chilling tale of their future.

The girls' excitement quickly turned to despair. Pointing at them with an unwavering stare, the woman declared:
"You will both be desolate—nobodies. It will be as if you never existed."

Devastated, the girls fled the house in tears. "It's not true," one cried, wiping her face. "Her prophecy is a lie. Don't listen to her!" But the other shook her head, sobbing. *"How can you say that? Everything she has said has come true. My life is over! Don't you see?"*

The two parted ways and returned to their homes.
One girl refused to accept the woman's words. Instead, she used them as fuel to pursue everything she dreamed of— determined to prove the prophecy wrong. Each day, the old woman's words reminded her of what she would not become. And when doubts tried to creep in, she declared:
"I am writing my own powerful narrative."

But the other girl clung to those words, replaying them over and over in her mind. She fully believed it was only a matter of time before the old woman's tale came true. Whenever she faced setbacks, she would whisper to herself, *"She was right, I am nothing."*

The years passed, and the two girls became women. The one who rejected the old woman's words grew into a powerful, successful leader. She often declared, "It was the failed prophecy of the old bag woman that made me the woman I am today."

The other woman, who embraced the prophecy as truth, watched it manifest in her life. Every failure, every missed opportunity, seemed to confirm the old woman's words. "She was right," she would say.

Was the old bag woman truly able to predict the future? No. She held no special power to see the unknown. Her power came from the belief people placed in her words. Because they believed, her predictions became self-fulfilling prophecies.

The same fate was promised to both girls, yet one lived a completely different outcome. The old woman's words never carried power on their own—it was the girls' belief that gave them weight. And, Sis, that's the same power belief holds in your life. What you agree with shapes what you experience. The question isn't what others are speaking over you; the question is, what are you agreeing to believe?

The Power of Self-Belief
What made the difference between those two girls? It wasn't the prophecy — it was the belief they fed. One fed self-doubt. The other fed self-confidence. And belief always produces fruit.

The old woman's words didn't dictate the future. One used them as motivation; the other let them define her fall. The power was in what they chose to believe. And the same is true for you.

So let me ask you: What beliefs are you feeding?

Because your mindset shapes everything — how you see yourself, how you face challenges, and how you pursue your goals. *Shift your mindset, and you'll shift your life.*

Here are three truths every unapologetic woman needs to remember:

Mindset Is Your Lens on Life
Your mindset is the filter on your future. It decides whether opportunities look possible or impossible. Change your lens, and you'll change what's visible.

Your Thoughts Drive Your Outcomes
Every action starts with a thought. Believe you're built for success, and your behavior will follow. Your mindset is the blueprint for your results.

Your Mindset Creates Your Reality
Your focus determines your future. A solution-driven, possibility-focused mindset uncovers doors you didn't even know were there.

Blind Spots That Hold You Back
Here are a few common things that stop us:

- **Comfort Zones:** Growth never happens in a comfortable place.
- **Negative Narratives**: Lies lose power the moment you stop rehearsing them.
- **Overthinking:** Doubt delays destiny. Move, even when the path isn't clear.
- **Comparison:** Your lane is your lane. Stay there. Win there.

The Weight You Don't Realize You Carry: Outdated beliefs will keep you grounded when God has called you higher. Let go of the false stories. Break the ceilings you built over yourself.

Overcoming Doubt and Stepping Into Your Power
Years ago, while life was handing me life-altering cards, I was on the brink of losing hope. I was desperately trying to believe that there was light at the other end of the tunnel.

I remember going to an appointment for assistance, and the woman's office cubicle was filled with positive affirmations and quotes. I pulled out my phone and hesitantly began snapping pictures. But as I continued, I became emboldened.

That moment lit a fire in me. I realized if I wanted change, I had to feed my mind something different.

When I left the appointment, I read those messages over and over again. I started searching for positive content. I began listening to motivational speakers, but these three quickly became my favorites: Lisa Nichols, Eric Thomas, and Les Brown.

In one of Les Brown's talks, he spoke about the intentionality of setting a positive mindset by starting and ending the day with uplifting stimuli while eliminating negative or harmful content from his mental diet. I adopted this practice and became purposeful about beginning and ending my day with 15 minutes of positive content that motivated, encouraged, and inspired me to embrace an empowered lifestyle.

What started as a 15-minute practice soon extended far beyond its original time frame. It reshaped my ambitions, sharpened my drive, and forced me to rethink my limitations.

The difference between bondage and breakthrough is what you choose to believe. That intentional thinking redefined the woman I was, shaped the woman I was becoming, and continues to set the standard for my future self.

Self-Work Activity

Now it's your turn to put this into practice. Empowered Mindset Practice: 15 Minutes to Start and End Your Day. Here's a powerful way to take control of your mind, your beliefs, and your destiny. Commit to 15 minutes at the start and end of each day to intentionally feed your mind positive, empowering content—and watch how your life begins to shift.

Step 1 – Create Your Mindset Space:
- Begin by eliminating content that sparks fear, worry, or doubt. This includes social media posts, negative news, or conversations that drain your energy.
- Instead, choose sources of inspiration: uplifting podcasts, motivational speakers, Scripture, affirmations, or videos that encourage and empower you.

Step 2 – Find a Support System:
- Seek someone to walk with you on this journey—a friend, family member, or mentor who speaks life into you.
- If no one is available, speak life into yourself. Stand in front of a mirror and declare a positive affirmation. Hear yourself say: "I can do this. I am capable. I am worthy."

Step 3 – Set the Tone for Your Day:
- Begin and end your day intentionally. Listen, read, or watch something that inspires hope, faith, and

Self-Work Activity

courage. Let these words shape your thoughts and **actions.**

Step 4 – Journal the Journey Write it down:
What fear or doubt showed up today?
How did my focus or affirmation shift it?
What win did I experience, big or small?

Step 5 – Declare Your Daily Affirmation
Morning and night, speak power over yourself:

"I am capable, worthy, and unstoppable."
"My past doesn't define my future."
"My power lies ahead, and I choose forward momentum."

Step 6 – Own Your Power
This is your daily declaration: no negative thought, no toxic person, no old wound gets to run your life anymore. Every time you feed your mind with positivity, you reinforce your confidence, your clarity, and your calling.

Chapter Seven

Move or Die Trying: The Cost of Staying Still

Hello Gorgeous.....

Affirmation:

Get out of your own way. The only one who can stop you is you

Growing up, I had a pet gerbil named Nicholas. He had everything—a cozy home, a wheel, and plenty of space. But no matter how hard he ran, he never got anywhere. Sound familiar? Sometimes we're just like Nicholas—busy, but stuck.

Stagnation is both an internal feeling of being trapped and the external result of avoiding necessary change or bold action. It's the sense of running in place—exerting energy but going nowhere. A cycle where effort is put in, yet progress is elusive. Stagnation isn't just the result of external forces; it's also a choice—a choice to stay safe, to let fear and uncertainty hold you back.

At times, life feels stagnant, with daily routines producing no decisive changes. Like Nicholas, we can get stuck. Often, fear is the culprit: fear of failure, fear of success, fear of the unknown. These fears trap us in a cycle where effort is put in, but nothing seems to change. Stagnation isn't just wasted effort—it's the refusal to move when movement is required.

Sis, this is your call to break free from both the internal resistance and the external barriers. Progress doesn't happen until you move. I've been there, desiring change, but refusing to act. Playing it safe feels risk-free, but it carries its own hidden costs: inaction and unrealized potential.

Staying still doesn't just delay you, it drains you. Every day you hesitate, your dreams lose oxygen. Every season you refuse to move, opportunities go by untouched. The cost of staying still is far greater than the cost of moving. The tragedy isn't in falling— it's in refusing to step.

Move or Miss Your Miracle
2 Kings 7:3-20 recounts the siege of Samaria, the capital of the northern kingdom of Israel, and the severe famine that followed. Four lepers sat at the city gate, realizing that staying put meant certain death. Their bold decision? Venture into the camp of the enemy, risking it all at the chance of survival.
 'If we say, "We will enter into the city, then the famine is in the city, and we shall die there: and if we sit here, we die also. Now therefore come and let us fall unto the host of the Syrians: if they save us alive, we shall live; and if they kill us, we shall but die.' (2 Kings 7: 4)."

The lepers' daring move paid off. They found the enemy camp deserted, filled with provisions. Their boldness not only saved their lives, but the fate of a nation. Like them, we must step beyond comfort, even when the outcome is uncertain. The act that feels risky may be the very thing that sets us free.

Complacency creeps in when we stay in familiar routines, minimizing risks, but blocking growth. Although we resist change, change is inevitable, and embracing it helps us to recognize the beauty in accepting the different seasons life often brings.

Here's an uncomfortable truth: Nothing changes if nothing changes.

Faith is Action

For years, I sat in stagnation. My dreams felt distant, my goals nonexistent. I was busy going nowhere, running hard like Nicholas on a treadmill—lots of effort, but no movement. Everything shifted the moment I dared to see differently. I created a vision board—not as decoration, but as a declaration. The power wasn't in the images themselves. It was how they forced me to see my future differently, to stare my goals in the face until they provoked me to move.

But a vision without execution is just a fantasy. I didn't stop at seeing—I built a plan. I mapped out SMART goals, step by step I executed. That's when the stagnation broke. That's when momentum showed up. The vision board gave me sight. The plan gave me movement. Execution gave me progress.

And let me tell you this: your circle matters just as much as your vision. On this road of becoming you need three women in your life—one beside you, one ten steps ahead, and one ten steps behind you. Collaborate with the one beside you. Serve and learn from the one ahead. Guide and support the one behind. If your circle doesn't challenge you, push you, pray for you, and call out your greatness, it's not your circle —it's your cage.

So I'll say it plainly: move, or die trying. Because the real death isn't failure, it's choosing to stand still while your purpose passes you by.

Transforming Setbacks into Runways for Success

As an EmpowerHER Strategist and coach, I equip women with three essentials: a clear path to an empowered lifestyle, the confidence to build thriving businesses and brands, and faith-driven platforms that silence fear and shatter limiting beliefs. True transformation demands a mindset shift, a solid action plan, and accountability. Are you ready to move? Remember— every action sets a reaction in motion. Your next step can shift everything.

Are you ready to move?

Here are 3 key takeaways from this chapter:

Fear Complacency: The choice to stay stuck is a powerful decision.

In the story mentioned above, the lepers reached a startling resolve. Staying in the place they had been for an undisclosed period of time was no longer acceptable. The act of doing nothing requires your permission to keep things just as they are. Had the men remained paralyzed by fear, they would have sentenced themselves and a nation to impending death. And just like the nation was waiting on the lepers, there may be someone waiting on you to make a bold move so they can be set free too.

Just Faith It — Sis: Faith is an action word. Don't fear the unknown—fear staying stuck in the same place for an indefinite amount of time. The obstacle that's blocking your blessing won't just disappear. You can't go around it. You can't go over it. You have to go through it. Faith-ing it means getting out of the boat, walking on water, stepping into the furnace, and leaping into the lion's dens. But here's an ugly truth: many of us fall short of blessings already within reach because we'll have to leave our comfort zones to get them.

Dreams Don't Pay Out If You Never Put Anything Down
The sports mantra that defines the way the game is played is: "Leave it all out on the field." While the stakes aren't life or death, this standard shapes players mindsets and drives how they approach the game.

How many of us have gone to sleep on our dreams, ideas, or goals? Sis, how long are you going to press the snooze button on your purpose? Leveling up isn't for the weak. I challenge you to level up anyway. Unrealized dreams can quickly transform into haunting nightmares.

As we close this chapter, face your fears and break free from complacency. Let go of whatever is holding you back from pursuing your dreams. Take bold steps towards your fullest potential. Remember, the journey isn't a sprint—it's a marathon. Stay committed, stay resilient, and stay focused. You have the power to defy failure, crush complacency, and ignite your purpose. *The cure for complacency is radical action. Your future depends on it. Move Sis, or die trying.*

Self-Work Activity

◆

Join the Unapologetically HER Podcast

The EmpowerHER Blueprint – She Said Yes Edition isn't just a series—it's a community. It's a space where I share my story, interview powerful women, and connect with change agents that motive and inspire. Together, we dive into real conversations, lessons, and testimonies that empower women to walk boldly in purpose.

The EmpowerHER Blueprint edition is where we'll go even deeper into the chapters of this book—unpacking insights, sharing takeaways, and bringing these principles to life in community.

Here's how you can connect:

- **Listen & Engage:** Tune in to the podcast, follow along on my social platforms, and join the conversation. Comment, share your takeaways, and let's build this community together.
- **Join Me On the Show:** When opportunities open, you'll be invited to pick three chapters that resonate with you most. We'll deep dive into your insights, lessons, and takeaways so your story can inspire other women walking this journey. If you're ready, email me at Shesaidyestoherself@gmail.com.
- **Stay Connected:** Follow me across Facebook, Instagram, TikTok, and LinkedIn at Chanelle Coleman Wesley for updates, behind-the-scenes moments, and new episodes.

This isn't just a podcast—it's a movement.

Chapter Eight

Beneath the Surface: Finding Hope Amid Difficult Roots

Hello Gorgeous.....

Empowering Proverb:

The roots of trauma can run deep, but they do not define the tree that grows above.

Trigger Warning: This chapter addresses sexual abuse and may stir memories of painful or traumatic experiences. My prayer is that it sparks the hard but necessary conversations that open the door to healing. Please read with care.

Pearls Don't Form Without Pressure
There is an intrinsic value in pearls—their creation mirrors how purpose often emerges from pain. Pearls form when unwanted substances, like grains of sand, enter an oyster.

The oyster's defense coats the irritant in layers, transforming it into something beautiful. The number of pearls enhances the oyster's value. Sis, your painful experiences can produce pearls too. God never allows pain without purpose. Even trauma, when surrendered, can birth something wonderfully exquisite.

Reflect: What "pearl" has emerged from a difficult experience in your life?

Uncovering What We'd Rather Bury

My baby girl Tarajah and I love to perform 'We Don't Talk About Bruno,' a song from Disney's Encanto. We sing it like it's nobody's business. But the message behind it hits deeper: families often silence the very truths that need to be spoken.

In the movie, a generational family lives in an enchanted home built from tragedy. The house gives magical powers to everyone except Mirabel, who's labeled a misfit, while Bruno's gift is despised. Why? Because it exposed truths the family didn't want to face. To avoid the negative narratives surrounding his gift, he withdrew, hiding behind the walls of the family home.

And just like that, the home and the family's gifts were on a fast track toward ruin. But everything shifted the moment Maribel dragged those uncomfortable truths into the light.

Fiction often imitates life. And if we're honest, many of us have lived this story too. We build walls in our minds, hiding traumatic experiences and painful events because they demand conversations we'd rather avoid—things we'd rather forget. Things that happened in our homes, churches, and schools, violations committed by strangers or, even more painfully, by people we trusted.

Sis, here's an ugly truth: What you bury alive doesn't die—it multiplies. If left unhealed, they resurface in ways that hold us back and keep us stuck. But when we confront them, we reclaim our power and transform what once wounded us into wisdom, strength, and purpose.

What truths are you avoiding that are keeping your gifts and healing hidden?

Turning Trauma Into Testimony
As a child, I learned that houses can give you special powers. Inside the walls of my family home I endured things that stripped me of my voice and forced my 4-to-5-year-old self to run naked up a flight of stairs, fleeing from my attacker. I detailed the events of this day in my first book, *Naked & Not Ashamed: The Transformational Devotional Experience.* That horrific event transformed my life. And in exchange, the gift my house gave me was becoming a Creative. I discovered the power of storytelling.

What tried to silence me ended up shaping my voice.
I saw how my story could produce pain, guilt, and shame. I watched it shock adults and terrify children, so I learned to stay silent. For years, I saw myself as a victim. But that narrative began to change when my Aunt Renata gave me a book that taught me I wasn't a victim—I was a survivor. My circumstances may have taught me silence, but they also revealed the power of release. Sharing my story showed me that my experience could ignite hope and resilience in others, becoming a survival guide for those navigating their own pain.

Share your story with a trusted friend, mentor, or spiritual leader—speaking the truth aloud strengthens your power over it.

If Your Walls Could Talk

If the walls in homes could talk, what stories would they tell? What gifts have your experiences given you? Your story, my story, our story—it's a plot twist only God could rewrite.

None of the pain in our stories is wasted, it carries purpose. It motivates, encourages, and empowers those battling life's challenges. God desires for us to share not just the good, but also the bad, the ugly, and the better parts of our journey. God said the weapons would form—but they wouldn't prosper. What the enemy meant for evil, God is working out for our good!

Your pain isn't stronger than your purpose. Lessons learned from difficult experiences position you to pivot — from the prison to the palace, from bondage to the promised land, and from the banks of the Red Sea to dry land. You will emerge from the depths of the fire to the executive office without smelling like smoke. You are not a victim; you are a survivor.

Write down one root issue you've avoided and one small step you can take this week to address it.

Sowing Seeds of Hope In Hard Soil

Growing up, my intergenerational family lived in a large three-story duplex. My grandmother took great pride in beautifying the exterior of our home. She pulled up what I thought were flowers, only for me to learn they were weeds. Dressed in a hat and gloves, with her tools and a bag beside her, she dug for what seemed like hours. Watching her, I asked, 'Grandma, may I help you?' She smiled, said yes, and showed me how to do the painstaking work.

I struggled, and soon noticed that when I tugged hard on the stems, they broke off, saving time and energy but leaving the roots in the ground. Proudly, I showed my grandmother my work. To my surprise, she looked disappointed. She placed her hand on my shoulder and said, "Chanelle, you've pulled off a lot of stems, but you didn't get the roots. Right now, both areas may look the same, but beneath the surface they're very different. If you only remove the stems, the weeds will grow back because the root remains. The root is hidden deep underground—it's what feeds the weed. But once the root is gone, the weed can't return.

At the time, I didn't fully understand. Weeks later, the area I had worked on alone was covered in new weeds. And once again, my grandmother was back at work.

Which patterns in your life are just surface-level fixes? What roots need to be exposed?

Resilience in the Rough: Turning Trials into Triumph
Forgive yourself for the things you did to survive traumatic experiences. Forgive those who hurt you—not because they're sorry or deserving, but because forgiveness is what frees you to grow. It's what you need to become healthy, happy, and whole. Your roots may stem from abuse, abandonment, illness, loss, rejection, neglect, discrimination, bullying, or more. Don't just pull off the stems—it's time to dig deep and expose the roots.

Do you want to be made whole? Healing is in the release. What you've survived has given you superpowers—strengths that can mend your broken pieces while inspiring others to rise from their pain. Embrace the gifts you were given; they came at a high price. They are your pearls. What hurt you can also heal you. And your story? It could be the survival guide someone else is waiting for.

This is My Prayer for YOU, Sis

Father God,
Today, I come before Your throne of mercy and grace on behalf of my Sister. You know her by name. You know why and how she gained her pearls. Cover her, I pray. Heal the places she doesn't talk about, the wounds hidden behind the walls, and restore what pain tried to steal. Let the very things meant to break her reveal the superpowers You placed inside her—strength, resilience, and a testimony that cannot be silenced.

Give her peace that surpasses all understanding. Breathe life into her dreams and aspirations. Remind her she is the head and not the tail, above only and not beneath, blessed in her coming in and in her going out. She was created to be a lender and not a borrower, a light that cannot be hidden, and a living witness of Your faithfulness.

Keep her forever in Your arms, and let her pearls shine as proof that what the enemy meant for evil, You have already turned for her good. I pray this prayer in the worthy name of Jesus. Amen.

Self-Work Activity

These next exercises are designed to help you reflect, heal, and grow. You don't have to do them all at once. Start with the activity that feels right for you in this season, and come back to the others when you're ready to go deeper. Healing is a journey, and every step counts.

1. **Map Your Tree**
Imagine yourself as a tree. Your actions are the fruit, but your roots—your beliefs and experiences—feed everything.

- What fruits are showing up on your branches?
- What roots are nourishing them?
- What did you uncover as you traced those roots back?

Activity: Draw your tree.

- **Roots:** label them with your difficult experiences and the lessons they left you.
- **Trunk:** write down your resilience, your strength, your character.
- **Branches:** show your gifts, accomplishments, and areas of growth.

Now reflect: Which branches need more sunlight—attention, nurturing, or pruning—to truly flourish?

2. **Write to Your Younger Self**
Look back at the little girl you once were.

- What advice would you give her?

Self-Work Activity

- What do you need to forgive her for?
- What victories have you accomplished that she never knew she'd live to see?
- Tell her why you're proud of her.

Close the letter by affirming her: You survived. You're still standing. And your story matters.

3. Expose a Root
Pick a difficult experience that still lingers.

- What emotions or beliefs are tied to it?
- How has it shaped your behaviors or decisions?
- What truth can you plant now that uproots the lie it left behind?

Final Reflection
Healing begins at the roots. Don't just trim what's visible—dig deep, confront what's hidden, and replace it with truth. Progress not perfection, is the goal. Every root you expose is a seed of freedom for you—and for the woman coming behind you.

Remember: Healing begins when we confront the roots of our struggles and work toward resolution. You are not alone on this journey—support is available, and your courage to face these roots will empower your growth and transform your story.

Chapter Nine

Goat Mode Activated: Stepping into Your Power and Potiental

Hello Gorgeous......

UNSTOPPABLE

Affirmation:

It's Me. It's My Time. It's My Turn.

G.O.A.T., the greatest of all time, it's a title every athlete wants, but only a few will possess. But G.O.A.T. is more than a title — it's a mindset. Let's explore our GOAT acronym.

G.O.A.T. Acronym
- G: God Said It's Yours — Go Get It.
- O: Outperform the Old You.
- A: Audacious Moves Only.
- T: Take the Leap.

Sis, this is the G.O.A.T. formula: Go after it, outperform the old you, make audacious moves, and take the leap. That's how greatness is built.

The acronym sets the playbook. Now it's time to run the drills. To see how these principles actually work, let's pull from two powerful examples: the athletes who dominate the arena and the goats who master the mountain. Both show us what it takes to level up and win.

Embrace Competition: G.O.A.T.s are fierce competitors. They thrive on competition and use it as fuel for growth. But Sis, your Sister isn't your competition, the only rival you've got is the woman you were yesterday. It's You vs You.

Focused Vision: G.O.A.T.s master both tunnel and peripheral vision, locked in on the goal, but sharp enough to spot opportunities and challenges along the way. Focused, aware, unstoppable.

Continuous Improvement: G.O.A.T.s never settle. They celebrate the win, but they refuse to live there. Growth is the goal, development is the standard, and domination is the result.

Resilience: G.O.A.T.s possess remarkable resilience, navigating adversity with the ability to bounce back from setbacks and failures. They see "setbacks" as opportunities to reposition, retool, and refocus. Every fall is fuel for the comeback.

Adaptability: G.O.A.T.s are flexible in the face of change, adjusting their approach to stay locked in on the goal. We can learn from this: Sis, if you don't like the way a chapter is going in your life, you don't have to stick to the script, turn the page.

Embrace Challenges: G.O.A.T.s don't run from adversity, they run through it. Every challenge is a stepping stone, every obstacle an invitation to elevate. What looks like resistance is really a setup for greatness.

Stay Humble: G.O.A.T.s stay grounded in the face of success, always recognizing there's room to grow. Sis, greatness is a journey, not a destination. Walk in humility, but don't shrink, own your greatness.

Embrace Failure: G.O.A.T.s understand that failure is part of the process, not the end of it. Every setback is a setup to learn, grow, and come back stronger. Refocus. Reset. Recommit.

Live in the Present: G.O.A.T.s master the now. They lock in on the moment, refusing to dwell on past wins or future worries. The power is in today.

Unwavering Commitment: G.O.A.T.s embody a steadfast commitment to their craft. Reaching the next level demands relentless effort. It's not about doing one move out of a hundred, it's about doing a hundred moves with unshakable consistency. They are driven, disciplined, and relentless in their pursuit. Consistency is the real flex.

These traits don't just belong to athletes on the big stage, or even to us when we're chasing our dreams. Sometimes, the best lessons on greatness come from the most unlikely places. Let me tell you about Henry, a little goat who proved what it really means to be G.O.A.T.

From Determination to Domination

The Tale of Henry, the Fearless Goat
Once upon a time, there was a brave little goat named Henry. He wasn't like the other goats; his legs were stunted, and he wasn't as strong, but what he lacked in size, he made up for in determination. At the top of Never Say Can't Mountain was a blackberry bush filled with the delicious berries, but to get it, goats had to navigate treacherous terrain and endure frigid temperatures. Only the bravest dared to try.

Henry was rarely picked to play with the herd. He was often teased, made fun of or overlooked. One day, Henry decided enough was enough and announced he'd do the unthinkable: he'd climb to the top of Never Say Can't Mountain and eat some of those delicious blackberries.

Too Small to Be Seen? Watch Me Work

"You can't climb to the top of Never Say Can't Mountain; it's too dangerous!" one goat said. "You're too little," chimed in another. "You're crazy; you'll never make it," laughed a third. Overhearing the commotion Henry's mother gently scolded him, "Henry, no one goes there. It isn't safe; you could get hurt. What would I do if something happened to you?"

Henry lowered his head and softly sighed. But that night, while everyone slept, he quietly left the safety of his herd and headed towards the mountain. The coyotes howled, but he remained undeterred. "I'm the bravest little goat on this side of Stony Rock Canyon," he told himself. As he climbed, he gazed at the beautiful hillside, but when he looked down, he saw the terrifying view below. "Don't look down; keep climbing Henry," he reminded himself.

Fear, Frustration, and Forward Motion

At sunrise, the herd realized Henry was gone. Everyone searched, but he was nowhere to be found. Henry's mother wanted to look for him on the mountain, but the herd persuaded her to think of her other children. No one dared go there; a rescue mission would likely end in tragedy. So they waited, hoping he'd return.

Hours turned into days, days into weeks, and weeks stretched into months. Winter came and went, leaving behind the promise of spring, but still no sign of Henry. Finally, the herd decided to commemorate his life. As they huddled together, sharing fond stories and expressing regret, they all began to cry.

One Step. One Victory. One Life Changed.
Suddenly, a young male goat wandered in, dragging a small vine heavy with blackberries. Its coat was gray with black streaks and splotches, twigs caught between its horns, scuff marks on its hooves, and its frame was a little on the smaller side.

"Why's everyone so sad?" the goat asked. "We've lost a brave little goat named Henry. He went up Never Say Can't Mountain, and no one's seen him since," a goat responded. Silence fell. Then the small goat dropped his vine of blackberries and lifted his head. "But I'm not dead. I'm alive. I'm the goat who learned to Never Say Can't!" "Henry!" his mother screamed. All the goats gathered around in excitement and disbelief. "You've grown, and look at your coat, it's changed," an older goat said. "Did you really make it to the top?" a small goat asked.

"Yes, I did. I traveled up the dangerous slopes, braved the fierce weather, navigated rough terrain, and encountered wild beasts. But I conquered them all, one step at a time. I heard so many voices telling me I couldn't do it, but I chose to listen to the one little voice deep inside me that told me I could!

Becoming the G.O.A.T.
Like Henry, I remembered that God said it was mine, so I had to go get it. I outperformed the old version of me, the one that doubted, feared, and second guessed, because she didn't have the final say over the woman I was becoming. I made audacious moves only, because settling was never part of the assignment. And when it came time for the leap, I took it, choosing faith over fear.

Sis, your mountain is waiting. What "Never Say Can't" mountain are you facing, and which bold step will prove your inner G.O.A.T.? Greatness isn't about size or strength; it's about the courage to climb when fear says stay still. One step. One decision. The mountain doesn't move for the fearful—it only gives way to those who dare to climb.

Self-Work Activity

◆

Journal Prompt: Step Into Your Power
Sis, it's time to stop playing small. This is where you activate
your G.O.A.T. mindset and step fully into your power—
whether in your career, your relationships, or that dream
you've been sitting on.

Journal Questions:

- *What's one bold move you've been too afraid to make, and
  what would happen if you did it today?*
- *Think back to a time you pushed through hardship. How did
  that moment of resilience shape the woman you are now?*
- *What challenge are you facing today that could be the very
  thing God uses to stretch and grow you?*

Take Action:
Don't just write it, move on it. Write down the exact steps
you'll take to push forward, and commit to one action today.
No excuses.

Engage with Like-Minded Women:
Iron sharpens iron. Share your reflections on social media,
tag the She Said Yes to Herself Unapologetically page, and use
#GoatModeActivated #SheSaidYesToHerself to inspire
another woman to rise. Connect with sisters on the same
journey, celebrate their wins, and let them celebrate yours.

Celebrate Your Progress:
Your progress is your proof. Every step, no matter how small,
is evidence that you're leveling up and stepping into your
greatness.

Chapter Ten

The Chinese Bamboo Tree

Hello Gorgeous.....

Positive Declaration:

Each morning, I want you to look at yourself in the mirror and say, "I may bend, but I won't break — watch me work!

Rooted in Persistence: The Power of Unseen Progress
A mentor to a group of adolescent girls walked to the front of the class and said, "Today marks the beginning of an invaluable lesson. This assignment will reveal the meaning of perseverance, resilience, and commitment. During this assignment, you will learn principles about others and the world around us. But most importantly, you will discover things about yourself. Not everyone will complete this journey; some of you will become distracted by the cares of life. Others will forfeit the lesson due to discouragement. And yet, another group will stick with the process and receive the prize."

Planting the Seeds: The Start of the Journey

The woman beckoned the girls forward to reveal the treasure she held in her hand. The little company crowded around, standing shoulder to shoulder, staring at her raised fist. Slowly, she opened it to reveal six tiny seeds in the palm of her hand.

"What's that?" one child asked, followed by another and another.

"This is the lesson I'm going to teach you; today, you will discover the parable of the Chinese Bamboo Tree."

Each girl excitedly selected a seed from her hand. "Follow me; we will plant them in the back of the school," she instructed. The girls eagerly raced behind the school to the lot out back. They planted the seeds in the ground and watered them. Within a few weeks, they raced to see if the seeds had started to sprout. But there were no results.

"Teacher, the trees aren't growing," one of the girls stated. "It takes time, be patient; it's growing," the mentor chided.

Waiting in Uncertainty: Weeks Turn into Months

Days passed, and the girls continued to water the seeds, but still, nothing broke through the soil.

"It's not working," one child remarked.

"Maybe we did something wrong," another suggested.

Still, the mentor advised them to faithfully attend to the task. Day in and day out, the little group toiled. Weeks turned into months. Finally, a year passed with no visible change. One by one, some girls grew tired of waiting and quit. Yet, a small remnant was left.

Faith in Action: Continuing Despite Discouragement
Two, then three years went by, and still no visible growth.
More students dropped away, discouraged. By the fourth year,
only two girls remained.
Frustrated, one finally collapsed in tears.

*"This is useless! It's not growing. I've done everything I could to
get it to grow, but nothing's worked!" she cried.*

*"Don't be discouraged; it's growing. Keep working. Commit to the
process. If you are diligent with the assignment, you will receive
an invaluable reward," the mentor admonished.*

*Frustrated, the young girl ran away in tears. Only the teacher and
one student remained.*

*The older woman looked intently into her eyes and asked, "Will
you leave too?"*

The girl quietly whispered, "No."

The Long Haul: Years of Care and Persistence
For four years, the young girl toiled over the tree with no
results. Anger, frustration, doubt, and disappointment filled
her days, yet she relentlessly cared for her Chinese Bamboo
Tree. Secretly, she began calling it the "Invisible Tree."

People mocked her, questioning why anyone in their right
mind would waste so much energy on such a pointless task.
Yet, with nothing more than a fragile thread of hope, she kept
watering, waiting, and believing.

Finally, the fifth year dawned. She was no longer a little girl but a young woman. Weary from the wait, heavy from hope deferred, she arrived at school ready to quit.

"I quit, I can't do this! I can't keep watering something I can't see," she told her mentor.

"But don't you want to see your tree?" the woman countered. "There wasn't anything yesterday, or the day before that, or the day before that. I doubt there will be anything different today," she argued.

"Come and see." The woman smiled, taking the young lady by the hand.

Breakthrough: The Invisible Becomes Visible
As she turned the corner, she froze. What had been buried for five years broke the surface in one night. Overwhelmed, she dropped to her knees, tears streaming down her cheeks as she beheld the sight of her Chinese Bamboo Tree, a tree that had miraculously sprung up overnight. Over the next five weeks, its height surpassed 90 feet. What had once been mocked in the dark now stood tall in the light, speaking loudly for all to see.

The Lesson: Growth Happens Beneath the Surface
The wise older woman asked, "So, do you think the tree grew over five weeks or five years?"

The young woman thought carefully.
"The answer is five years. The tree began growing the moment it was planted, but its growth happened beneath the surface, hidden from sight. Its maturity wasn't achieved in just days or weeks of watering; it was the result of years of nurture, marked by sweat, tears, disappointment, and frustration.

The mentor nodded. "Exactly. Investments of this magnitude don't yield results overnight. They require consistent nurturing, watering, seeding, and planting. The initial costs are high, with little to no return at first, but over time, the payoff is tremendous. Your 'Invisible Tree' is undeniable proof."

Self-Reflection
- Think about a time when you poured effort into something without seeing any change. How did you stay consistent?
- Who or what has left you feeling alone in your journey, and how did you keep going anyway?
- What invisible tree in your life needs patience, faith, and consistency to bloom?

Patience in Growth: Nurturing Success Over Time
Sis, the journey to success mirrors the growth of the Chinese Bamboo Tree. The effort we invest in building our businesses, pursuing our callings, or developing ourselves often feels like the early stages of this remarkable tree—slow, hidden, and frustrating.

We want quick results. We want to see fruit right away. And when we don't, discouragement creeps in. But here's the truth: just because you don't see anything yet doesn't mean nothing's happening. Growth always starts underground.

So let me ask you: do you have the grit to keep showing up when it feels like nothing's moving? Will your faith remain steady when the evidence looks silent? Don't let the silence fool you—your seed is working, your roots are stretching, and your season is closer than you think.

The one who refuses to stop watering will always be rewarded. Stay planted. Stay patient. Trust the process.

Breakthrough After Delay: The Bamboo Tree Lesson

The steps you're taking today are sowing into your tomorrow. Giving up is not an option. Let's break down the truths this tree teaches us:

- **Patience and Persistence:** Growth takes time. If you stop watering, you forfeit the harvest.
- **Rooted Foundation:** Shallow roots can't survive storms. Strong roots will hold you through anything.
- **Unseen Growth:** Just because it's invisible doesn't mean it's inactive. What looks delayed is still developing.
- **Resilience and Flexibility:** Like bamboo, bend but don't break. Flexibility is strength in motion.

Reflections and Empowerment

Sis, let me break this all the way down for you:

- **Delayed does not mean denied.** Silence in your season doesn't mean God forgot you, it means He's preparing you for a breakthrough.
- **You can't microwave destiny.** Some things only bloom in the slow cooker of faith, time, and persistence.
- **Don't quit in year four.** The miracle you're waiting for might be hiding in tomorrow's obedience.
- **Roots before fruit.** If you don't go deep in private, you'll never stand tall in public.
- **Convenience won't crown you.** Commitment will. Crowns are reserved for the women who stay planted.

Sis, this parable is proof that God's timing is perfect and His calling is unshakable. What He plants, He waters. What He starts, He finishes. Your growth isn't for the world's approval—it's for His assignment. Greater is He that is in you than anything standing against you. So even when it looks silent, trust this: if God spoke it, it's already in motion. The roots are working, the season is shifting, and the bloom is inevitable.

Sometimes we want to pick the soil we grow in. We want to choose the seed and the season. But that's not our call—it's God's work. Unapologetically bloom where He planted you.

Self-Work Activity

Bamboo Growth Challenge: Seeds of Success Project
Mustard seeds are among the smallest seeds in existence, yet they grow into mighty, fully developed trees. Like those seeds, your dreams are meant to follow a similar growth pattern—starting small but filled with infinite potential.

Join the Bamboo Growth Challenge- Here's how to participate:

1. **Gather Your Materials:** You'll need a small glass jar or container, soil, mustard seeds, decorative items like affirmations, images, decorative paper, rhinestones, etc.
2. **Make It Yours:** Decorate your jar with words, decorative paper, rhinestones, images, etc., that reflect your personality, goals, and aspirations. Let it inspire you.
3. **Plant Your Foundation:** Fill your container with soil, plant a few seeds, and place it in a sunny spot.
4. **Water with Intention:** Care for your seeds, using this time to reflect on your personal growth, dreams, and goals.
5. **Watch the Process:** Growth requires patience, and your 'Bamboo Tree' will teach you just that. Over time, as the plant outgrows its jar, you'll see how your dreams—when nurtured— can no longer be contained.
6. **Document Your Journey:** Keep a journal nearby to capture your thoughts, emotions, and progress. Write about moments of doubt and celebrate even the smallest victories. Your reflections will show your growth.
7. **Share Your Growth.**
   Your journey is bigger than you—share your jar on Instagram by tagging me @Chanelle Coleman Wesley

Together, we'll create a ripple effect of empowerment, faith, and inspiration.

Chapter Eleven

Just Faith It

Hello Gorgeous.....

Scripture:

"For as the body without the spirit is dead. Faith without works is dead."

The Obstacle Before the Promise
As the Israelites approached the Jordan River to enter the Promised Land, they faced a formidable obstacle. At that time of year, the river was too high for a safe crossing, creating a barrier to receiving the promise. On the riverbank, it was clear— they couldn't go over or around it. Success required going through it.

Faith in Action: Practical Steps to Build Your Trust
In preparation for what the Lord was preparing to do, they cleansed themselves and renewed their commitment to Him. But the river wasn't the only obstacle. Their

inheritance was already occupied by inhabitants who weren't about to give up their territory without a fight. Crossing the Jordan wasn't just about reaching land — it was about announcing to the nations that the God of Israel was faithful, present, and powerful enough to deliver His people. These acts would give undeniable proof that God Himself had given the land and the nations into their hands.

The Step of Faith
The Lord instructed Joshua to command the priests to carry the Ark of the Covenant into the waters. Once the priests reached the middle of the river, each tribe was told to send one man to collect a large stone from the riverbed and bring it to the other side. Those stones would become a memorial of God's power.

But don't miss this: the waters didn't move until the priests stepped in. As soon as their feet touched the edge, the river parted. Faith moved what strength and human ability could not. The same God who split the Red Sea now parted the Jordan—reminding Israel then, and us now, that the God of their past is the God of their present. And hear me clearly: He's still parting waters today. Circumstances may change, but God never changes —He's still God."

The Stones of Remembrance
Those who had crossed the Red Sea as children now stood as witnesses to this new miracle. God had carried them through the wilderness, and now He was carrying them through the Jordan. The twelve stones gathered from the riverbed stood as a memorial — not just for them but for every generation that would come after, a testimony of God's favor, His faithfulness, and His unmatched power.

Beyond the Seen: Walking Boldly in Unshakable Faith
A move of God demands radical faith. Radical faith will require you to do the unconventional. We want the miracle, but fear stepping into the water because we're afraid we might get wet. Sis, you can't see God move if you never move. Faith is not a spectator sport. You can't stand on the sidelines and expect breakthroughs. The Jordan wasn't just their river — it's our reminder that faith requires action.

Faith doesn't wait for proof — it walks on water.

Here's an uncomfortable truth Sis: the miracle isn't delayed by God's power — it's delayed by your refusal to take the first step.

That's the power of faith in action, it moves obstacles that human effort never could. But don't just read this as inspirational story; it's our playbook. The Jordan holds lessons for us, and if you'll grab hold of them, they'll change the way you walk into your next season. Here are eight keys that will anchor your faith when the waters rise.

Taking the Leap: 8 Key Principles of Faith
- **Faith is developed under pressure**. Stop begging God to take the weight off. That trial isn't punishment, it's preparation. Pressure produces endurance, and endurance produces strength.
- **Faith requires movement.** You can't just believe and stand still. Real faith demands obedience and action. Believing alone isn't enough, you've got to move.
- **Carry mementos with you.** The twelve stones weren't just rocks; they were receipts. Testimonies are proof that if He did it before, He'll do it again. What's your memorial?

Write it down. Rehearse It.
- **Obedience unlocks miracles.** Miracles live on the other side of instructions. Even when what God says seems unconventional, trust Him. Obedience always opens doors.
- **Believe the promises of God**. If He said it, He'll perform it. The victory is already yours. Stop wrestling with doubt and start walking like it's already done.
- **Recognize the power of collective faith**. Israel didn't cross alone. Joshua led, the priests stepped, the people followed. Who you walk with matters. Don't isolate yourself, community strengthens faith.
- **Faith is a journey, not a shortcut.** It's stepping into the unknown with trust that God has already made provision. Faith isn't fast food, it's the long road that leads to destiny.
- **Trust God's timing.** The water didn't move until their feet touched it. Your miracle isn't waiting on His ability, it's waiting on your step.

Sis, your Jordan may not be a river, but it's real. It may be your fear, your doubt, your finances, or the weight of your past. But just like Israel, your breakthrough is on the other side of obedience. The waters don't part until you move.

So take the step. Get your feet wet. Trust His timing. Lean into His promises. And watch God make a way where there was no way.

Self-Work Activity

Take a moment to reflect and write down five "memorial moments" in your life — your personal evidence of God's hand at work. Then, write a thank-you letter to God, expressing gratitude for the blessings and favor He has commanded over your life.

Chapter Twelve

The Exodus: From Bondage to Breakthrough

DELIVERANCE

Hello Gorgeous......

Scripture:

I refuse to return to the spaces or places that I had to pray my way out of.

From Bondage to Freedom

Bondage. Merriam-Webster defines it as being bound by compulsion. For Israel, it meant over 400 years of chains, whips, and suffering in Egypt. But before the chains ever formed, God had already spoken. He swore to Abraham, childless at the time, that his descendants would fall prey to bondage for a season, but the promise wouldn't die there. When Israel emerged from slavery they would outnumber the stars and inherit a land flowing with milk and honey.

Centuries later, when the cries of His people pierced the heavens, God raised up Moses and shook Egypt and the world. And when He brought Israel out, they didn't walk out as slaves, they marched out as a mighty nation.

Centuries later, when the cries of His people pierced the heavens, God raised up Moses and shook Egypt and the world. And when He brought Israel out, they didn't walk out as slaves, they marched out as a mighty nation. They didn't leave Egypt empty, they left drenched in grace, covered in favor, and carrying the spoils of their enemies.

God's promise wasn't just about freedom; it was about identity. They weren't leaving bondage to wander. They were stepping into covenant. Into abundance. Into a testimony that every nation would see and fear: the God of Heaven fights for His people, and when He speaks a promise, not even 430 years of chains can cancel it.

The Enemy We Serve
Just as Pharaoh stood as the oppressor of Israel, Satan stands as the oppressor of humanity.

Pharaoh's chains bruised the body, but Satan's chains crush the soul, enslaving us inside an invisible prison without walls.

Pharaoh bound Israel with chains; Satan binds us with sin.
Pharaoh's whip broke bodies; Satan's lies break identities.
Pharaoh decreed death over their sons; Satan schemes destruction over our souls.
Pharaoh hardened his heart against God; Satan twists hearts to rebel against God.
Pharaoh refused to let God's people go; Satan refuses to release anyone who bows to sin.

Sin is the master, the chain, the prison. And Satan uses sin as his greatest weapon to keep us bound.

But here's the truth: Pharaoh was not Israel's true master, and Satan isn't ours. The Word says whoever we yield ourselves to obey becomes our master (Romans 6:16).

Yet just as Egypt could not hold Israel, sin cannot hold those

God has declared free. The same Deliverer who broke Pharaoh's grip has placed Satan under His feet. Who the Son sets free is free indeed (John 8:36).

From Bondage to Freedom: Steps Toward Deliverance
God dismantled Egypt plague by plague, showing His supremacy over every idol they trusted:

Water Turned to Blood – Hapi (the Nile god): Egypt's lifeline became death. What they trusted to give life failed them.
Application: *Anything you drink from outside of God will leave you empty. Only He satisfies.*

Frogs – Heqet (fertility goddess): Their idol overran their homes. What they worshiped became their torment.
Application: *What you tolerate will multiply until it steals your peace.*

 Lice/Gnats – Geb (earth god): Dust became chains. God used the lowliest thing to expose their false gods.
Application: *Small compromises today become shackles tomorrow.*

Flies – Khepri (fly god): Swarms filled Egypt, but not Goshen. God marked His people with protection.
Application: *When God covers you, nothing can touch what belongs to Him.*

 Livestock – Hathor (cow goddess): Their wealth collapsed in a single blow, but Israel's herds were untouched.
Application: *Whatever you depend on more than God will eventually fail you.*

Boils – Sekhmet and Imhotep (healing gods): Their false healers couldn't save them. Only God could.
Application: *God exposes false sources so only He gets the glory.*

Hail – Nut (sky goddess): Fire and ice fell from the sky, striking Egypt but sparing.
Application: *What you thought would cover you may be the very thing God uses to break you.*

Locusts – Seth (god of storms): Everything left was devoured. Yet again, God protected His own.
Application: *Refusing to release what isn't yours will destroy everything around you.*

Darkness – Ra (sun god): Egypt's greatest deity was silenced. Darkness fell, but Israel had light.
Application: *When the true Light shows up, every false light is exposed—don't let your life depend on anything that dies when the switch flips.*

Death of the Firstborn – Pharaoh (worshiped as a god): Believed to be a life giver and sustainer. The power of life and death belongs to God. There was no safety outside of the blood of the Lamb.
Application: Application: *We are saved by grace through faith in Jesus Christ. When the plagues fall, God promises they will not touch those who are covered by the blood of the Lamb.*

The writing was on the wall. Egypt and its false systems of worship were exposed. Pharaoh had no choice but to release what God had already declared free.

And when Israel walked out, they didn't walk out empty. They walked out drenched in grace, covered in favor, and carrying the spoils of their enemies. God tore down Egypt's false gods, stripped Pharaoh of power, revealed Israel's true Deliverer, and declared, *"I Am God, and besides Me, there is no other."*

But unfortunately, Israel carried the residue of slavery in their hearts. Though their bodies were free, their minds still rehearsed the lies of the past. It's hard to believe, but after centuries of being enslaved they begged to return to bondage, because it felt safer than the path of freedom God was calling them to (Numbers 11:4-6, Numbers 14:3-4). Let's face it, it was what they knew.

Sound familiar? Many of us live the same way. We call it tradition, culture, or "just the way it is." But let's be real—it's bondage dressed up in family patterns.

Your grandmother fell into the trap of silence when she should have spoken. Your mother carried that same weight, settling when she should have soared. And now, without even realizing it, you've been pulled into the same cycle — repeating patterns you were never meant to inherit.

That's not inheritance. That's a curse. And curses only stop when we boldly declare, "It ends with me."

Sis, Egypt is not your destiny. Bondage is not your portion. Bondage is not your identity. God called you to be the chain breaker for generations coming behind you.

Girl, You're Free
Israel didn't just leave Egypt; they left bondage. You've got to do the same.
Don't just shout about freedom—walk in it.
Name your Egypt. Confront your Pharaoh. Burn your idols.

And with the authority that comes to you as a Daughter of God through Jesus Christ, decree and declare it in the heavens and in the earth:
"I will not stay bound. I'm crossing over!"

Self-Work Activity

◆

Confronting and Canceling Your Egypt

Sis, we can leave Egypt, but Egypt doesn't always leave us. This exercise is about silencing the lies we tell ourselves and walking fully in the liberty of being Daughters of the Most High.

Grab a few sheets of paper, a red pen, a black pen, and a pencil. This is not busywork, Sis—this is warfare.

Name Your Bondage

Write down the experiences God has delivered you from in black ink. Don't dress it up. Don't water it down. Call it what it was.

Expose the Lies

Egypt will whisper fairytales to keep you bound. Write those lies in pencil—because lies don't last, and they're about to be erased.

Declare the Truth

For every lie, counter with the truth in red ink. Red represents covenant, victory, and the blood of the Lamb. Let the truth ring louder than every lie.

Cancel the Lie

Erase every false narrative you wrote in pencil. Watch them disappear. That's what happens when truth shows up— bondage has to bow.

Keep Your Freedom in Sight

Place your truth list where you can see it. Read it. Speak it. Believe it. Let it remind you daily that Egypt is behind you and freedom is your portion.

Sis, don't just complete the exercise—walk in it. Because every erased lie is proof that God has called you out of bondage into His marvelous light.

Chapter Thirteen

The Exodus: Walking Boldly into Your Promised Land

Hello Gorgeous.....

Scripture:

I am no longer bound by what tried to break me. I can't be held by what God has already set me free from.

Let's Get Real,
A stronghold isn't just a fortress—it's a prison of the mind and spirit. It's built brick by brick through lies, generational patterns, and demonic influence. Its purpose? To keep you from walking into the freedom God already promised.

Paul reminds us: "For the weapons of our warfare are not carnal, but mighty through God to the pulling down of strongholds." (2 Corinthians 10:4)

I watched a viral clip of a women's conference where a popular minister declared, "Strongholds are for strong women... we

need something stronger than what's holding us."
The crowd erupted in applause.

Listen closely, do you hear the trap in that? Without realizing it, they were co-signing bondage instead of breaking free.

A stronghold is anything that has a strong hold on you.

Depression. Addiction. Trauma. That fear. That insecurity. That relationship you keep running back to. The enemy specializes in blurring the lines—convincing us to see liberty as bondage while calling captivity freedom. A master, he will have us shouting amen to the very thing that holds us hostage.

God's Promise in Advance
For Israel, bondage meant over 400 years of chains, whips, and suffering in Egypt. But before a single chain ever formed, God had already spoken. Swearing to Abraham, childless at the time, that his descendants would fall prey to bondage for a season, but the promise wouldn't die there. Israel would emerge, outnumbering the stars in the sky, and inherit a bountiful land flowing with milk and honey.

They didn't leave bondage to wander. They walked into a covenant. Into abundance. Into a testimony that every nation would see and fear: Jehovah fights for His people, and when He speaks a promise, not even 430 years of chains can cancel it.

The Enemy We Serve
Pharaoh's chains bruised the body, but Satan's chains destroyed souls. Satan hardened Pharaoh's heart, using him to mirror his obsession with keeping people bound, but his reach extends far beyond Egypt. Pharaoh stood as the oppressor of Israel, but Satan stands as the oppressor of humanity.

Pharaoh's whip bruised bodies, Satan's whip breaks souls. Pharaoh killed their infant sons, Satan crushes generations. Pharaoh refused to let Israel go. Satan refuses to let go of humanity.

Scripture says whoever you yield to becomes your master (Romans 6:16).

Satan desires to keep us bound, chained in the prison house of sin. But Pharaoh was never Israel's true master—and Satan isn't ours. The Deliverer who crushed Pharaoh's grip has already placed Satan under His feet. Egypt could not hold Israel and sin cannot hold those God has declared free.

Who the Son sets free is free indeed. (John 8:36)

The Exodus: A Test of Faith
Egypt was the embodiment of a stronghold. As each plague unfolded, the hopes of the Israelites rose and fell with Pharaoh's repeated promises to release them, but then he'd abruptly change his mind. But in the darkest hour, right before their breakthrough, the anticipation of freedom was palpable. After this final scourge, Pharaoh would be forced to submit. God ensured that their last night in Egypt would be one to remember. God was setting the stage for the ultimate showdown.

At its center was the lamb, a symbol of Jesus Christ and His coming sacrifice, which would do more than free Israel. His life, death, burial, and resurrection would emancipate the world from the bondage of sin.

Faith in Motion
The cost of the ransom was clear: **the Innocent had to die to rescue those in bondage.** The Passover feast required the

sacrifice of a young male lamb, spotless and without blemish. Its blood was applied to the doorposts of the home.

This sacrificial feast foreshadowed the death of the true Lamb of God who takes away the sins of the world.

Every household faced a choice—stay uncovered and die, or apply the blood and live.

And just as they had a choice then, we have a choice now: put the blood of the Lamb on the doorposts of your heart and live, or remain uncovered and die.

The Significance of the Lamb

Lamb can be a succulent meal, when you choose how it's prepared, the cuts, and spices. But the Passover didn't allow that. The lamb roasted whole was prepared with bitter herbs, reminding partakers of the bitterness of bondage. Every part was to be eaten, nothing wasted, including the less-than-savory portions. Any remains were burned. This communal meal carried profound purpose.

The Father's gift to Israel and the world is freedom from bondage through His Son Jesus Christ. But that freedom came at a considerable price— it demanded the life, death, and resurrection of the *Son of God*. A debt that God emptied heaven to pay.

The good news about Jesus Christ is meant to be shared with everyone. Just as God established His covenant with Israel, He has established a new covenant with us. During Passover, once the blood was applied, no one was allowed to go in or out of the house—and likewise, God doesn't want us drifting in and out of relationship with Him.

Israel don't get to pick and choose which parts of the lamb to eat then, and we can't pick and choose which parts of His commandments and precepts to obey now. With God, it's all or nothing.

The Meaning of the Passover Feast

The Passover feast marked Israel's final hours of slavery and the dawn of their liberation—a night both bitter and beautiful. Faith-fueled obedience signaled the death angel to pass over, sparing their firstborn. God refused to leave a revolving door back into bondage. The blood of the Lamb was their covering, their protection, their unmistakable sign of freedom. Once the blood was applied to the doorposts, the people were sealed in until daybreak. There was no safety outside the blood of the Lamb. And at dawn, Pharaoh, who had mocked their God and hardened his heart, was forced to release them. They walked out of Egypt truly free, fully covered, and ready to step into their promised life.

Sis, hear me: *the same God who broke Pharaoh's grip is still breaking chains today. Just as the blood of the Lamb shielded Israel, when you place the blood of Christ on the doorposts of your heart, you are covered, sealed, and set free to walk in life, victory, and purpose. Nothing can touch what God has covered. Nothing can stop what He has ordained. The blood still works— and it still speaks.*

This isn't just history; it's your invitation. Apply the blood to every fear, every failure, every generational curse. Stay inside His covering. Don't step in and out of truth. When the blood is on you, freedom isn't a wish—it's a guarantee.

God understands mankind's tendency to romanticize abusive and toxic relationships, and our ability to alter narratives until we start fantasizing about our captor or our time in bondage. He wanted this meal to leave a bitter taste in their mouths. The bitterness wasn't just symbolic, it was intentional, designed to break their emotional ties to captivity and serve as a constant reminder of why returning wasn't an option.

Romanticizing Bondage

Even after their miraculous escape, Israel repeatedly rehearsed a false story about their years in Egypt. They spoke of the "good food" and "easier days," conveniently forgetting the whips, forced labor, and cries for deliverance. Freedom felt uncertain, so bondage began to look familiar, and even desirable (Numbers 11:4-6, Numbers 14:2-4).

Shake our heads in disbelief all we want, but if we're honest, we're not so different. God delivers us from crisis after crisis, yet we flirt with captivity. God doesn't want to drag us kicking and screaming out of bondage because we've developed a fondness for our captor.

While we may not be slaves to a physical taskmaster, we can be bonded to a person, place, thing, or idea, and that enslavement can be just as deadly and cruel as any tyrannical master.

Embrace the Bitter with the Sweet

A word of caution, Sis: embrace the bitter with the sweet! Just as God allowed bitterness on the Israelites' last night in Egypt, don't despise or forget the bitterness in your own experiences. These moments remind you not to return to the circumstances you prayed your way out of. God can bring you out of bondage. He overthrew a nation to free His people, and He'll do the same for you.

If you're in bondage, don't give up. The darkest hour is just before daybreak. You may not be freed the first, second, or third time, but your change is coming. Expect a breakthrough.

The Urgency of Now: Delays Can Interrupt Your Exodus
God commanded them to eat standing, fully dressed, with staff in hand. They prepared in anticipation of breakthrough. They did not wait for the announcement. They acted in faith. Sis, faith packs before the doorbell rings. It believes before it sees.

The Israelites were told to stay ready because God knew Pharaoh's pattern. Though the final plague would force him to release them, his heart would harden again. A single delay on their part would have cost them the promise. The command was clear: **Be ready to move the moment freedom calls.**

This is your wake-up call. Pray with your boxes packed, keys and purse in hand, heels on, and prayer list ready. Don't wait for the "perfect time." Prepare now. Faith isn't passive—it moves while the ink on the miracle is still wet.

Preparation for Breakthrough
The urgency of readiness is God's reminder to stay vigilant. Just as Israel had to be ready to leave Egypt at a moment's notice, you must stay prepared for God's intervention in your life. The calling and the anointing on your life will never permit bondage. By the power of the Spirit, your weapons dismantle lies, disrupt patterns, and break strongholds. You are not fighting for victory—you are fighting from victory.

God overthrew a nation to free His people, and He will do the same for you. When He says "move," hesitation can cost you the door He's opening. Stay ready. Stay dressed. Stay packed.

Praise in the Hallway – The Victory Stance
Breakthrough isn't just about the exit; it's about the posture you take while you wait. Sis, God is alive. He is not dead. God's

Word breathes life over you. The blood still works. What covered Israel covers you. Favor is on you. Favor is not fair, but it is yours.

So don't wait until you see the doors swing open to praise. Praise Him in the hallway. Lift your hands before the chains fall. Dance before the email arrives. Worship before the answer comes. The same God who spoke freedom over Israel speaks freedom over you. What He starts, He is faithful to finish.

Sis, when God opens the door, don't pause to negotiate with what He's already defeated.
Leave the chains, leave the crumbs, leave the conversations that keep you small.
Step into freedom with your head high and your heart unshaken —because what's behind you can't compete with what's waiting ahead.

Walk out of Egypt and never look back.

Self-Work Activity

◆

Self-Work: Walk Your Journey Challenge
If these shoes could talk! No one will ever truly know what it's been like to walk a mile in your shoes. But today, we're sharing a piece of our stories.

Step 1 – Show Off Your Shoes
Snap a photo of yourself wearing your favorite pair of shoes while holding this book.

Step 2 – Share Your Story
In your caption, reflect on the significance of those shoes in your journey—your challenges, growth, and triumphs. Let the world see what these shoes represent in your life.

Step 3 – Spread the Inspiration
Post your photo and caption on Instagram, Facebook, X, TikTok, or LinkedIn. Use the hashtags below to connect with others and celebrate your unique shoe stories.
Tag @ChanelleColemanWesley so I can celebrate with you!

Step 4 – Pass the Baton
Think of a woman with an inspiring story. Tag her in your post, challenge her to read this chapter, and invite her to share a photo with her favorite shoes, this book, and her story.

I can't wait to read your stories and see those shoes, Sis. I'll be watching the tags and leaving comments.

Hashtags to Use
#SheSaidYesToHerselfUnapologetically
#IAmReleasingWhatNoLongerAligns
#RedDesignerShoeChallenge

Chapter Fourteen

Red Designer Shoes

OUTGROW

Hello Gorgeous.....

Affirmation:

I no longer chase what doesn't serve me—
I release what no longer fits and boldly
make room for what's rightfully mine.

Love at First Try

Walking through downtown, a stunning pair of red
designer heels caught her eye. Captivated, she stepped
inside and asked the cashier about the expensive, limited-
edition shoes. The store only had one pair left. The shoes
were outside of her budget, but she tried them on anyway.

The moment her feet slipped into the heels, it was love at
first try! The shoes hugged the contours of her feet
perfectly. She paced in front of mirrors feeling beautiful,
powerful, and unstoppable. Every eye in the store followed
her, admiring the elegance and confidence the heels
seemed to give her. There was no sense in denying it. She
adored the shoes.

The Price of the Swipe

Just then, another woman approached the cashier asking about the same shoes. The urgency struck—if she didn't buy them now, she'd lose her chance. She pulled out her credit card and purchased them, deciding that some opportunities could not wait.

The red pumps instantly became her signature shoes. She wore them everywhere—dinner parties, receptions, nights out, weddings, funerals. No matter the event, compliments followed her, and she secretly loved the validation.

But time brought change. Her feet gradually grew, something her other shoes could accommodate—but not the red pumps. Regrettably, she wouldn't find this out until the next event. Weeks later, she prepared for the city's most anticipated event, fabulously dubbed "The Party of the Century."

Forcing It to Fit

It took over three hours for her to get ready: shower, shave, fix her hair, apply makeup, and slip into her little black dress. Finally, it was time for her to slip on her favorite heels...but they didn't fit.

Panicked, she tried everything—stretching, adjusting, coaxing her feet into the pumps—but nothing worked. Time was against her, and her friend arrived. **She had two choices:** *pick another pair or squeeze her feet into the shoes. What did she do? She stuffed her feet into the red pumps and headed out.*

Pain in Plain Sight

The night was long and painful. Circling for parking, walking long city blocks, climbing staircases, and attempting to mingle and dance, the shoes punished her with every step.

By the end of the night she had spent most of the evening at the beautifully decorated table, her feet throbbing in pain, while everyone else enjoyed the event into the early hours of the morning.

When she returned to her apartment, she was exhausted. Her feet throbbed with excruciating pain. Pumps in hand, she hobbled inside, letting the shoes fall clumsily to the floor. She made a beeline for the tub, sinking into a long, hot bath while massaging her aching feet.

An hour passed, and she finally emerged, her eyes fell on the shoes as she walked through the room. They were gorgeous— but were they worth all of the pain and discomfort they had caused? Deep down, she knew they didn't fit. It was time to let them go. But she had tied her identity to the status of owning them, and with the hefty price she'd paid, she was reluctant to give that up without a fight.

From Desire to Detachment
The following day, she called the store where she had purchased the shoes, hoping for a remedy, but they were no help. Next, she turned to the internet, searching for tricks and quick fixes. Nothing worked. Buying an identical pair was out of the question. Stubbornly, she made three more attempts to wear the shoes, clinging to the hope that miraculously things would be different. But each time, she suffered for it. Finally, she made the reluctant decision to donate them.

This shoe journey could easily mirror some relationships. There are connections that are doomed from the start. Yet we ignore the red flags, choosing to fixate on feelings rather than principles that reveal uncomfortable truths.

The Truth About Growth
Growth is necessary. As we develop, sometimes growth

brings us closer to those we are connected with; other times, it drives us apart. Too often, we resist this reality. We try to ignore the change or learn to live with discomfort. We squeeze ourselves into spaces we've already outgrown. *The truth is—we've grown in ways the relationship can no longer accommodate.*

The Cost of Holding On
The connection has served its purpose and can no longer contain all that we bring to the table. The longer we stay in that space, the more unnecessary pain, aggravation, and frustration we will feel. After exhausting every possibility to resolve the issues, we are left with a choice: keep the relationship or end it. Too often we obsess over what we might lose if we let go, instead of considering what we're destined to gain. So we keep forcing what no longer fits—trying to make room for what God is already calling us to release.

In this season, Sis, I need you to promise me one thing: that you will stop pouring into people, places, things, or mindsets that no longer serve you. Don't expect others to extend themselves beyond their capacity to give.

Don't let misplaced loyalty keep you in spaces that common sense should have removed you from.

Just as the woman in the story had to accept that her beloved red designer pumps no longer fit, there are times we must recognize when certain mindsets, relationships, or environments no longer align with our growth or well-being. Continuing to invest your energy, time, and resources into stagnant spaces only leads to pain, frustration, and stagnation.

Let It Go

Holding on to what no longer fits prolongs discomfort and deepens struggle. Forcing ourselves into situations, relationships, or mindsets that no longer serve us or are purpose doesn't just cause temporary discomfort, it chips away at our peace, progress, and potential. The more we insist on staying in places we've outgrown, the more our sense of self-worth and direction diminishes.

When a person, place, thing, or idea cannot give you what you need to be healthy, happy, and whole, it's your responsibility to align with what does. Let it go, Sis.

Some relationships are breathtaking in the window but brutal on the walk—beautiful to look at, but painful to live in.

Self-Work Activity

◆

Self-Work: Walk Your Journey Challenge

If these shoes could talk! No one will ever truly know what it's been like to walk a mile in your shoes. But today, we're sharing a piece of our stories.

Step 1 – Show Off Your Shoes

Snap a photo of yourself wearing your favorite pair of shoes while holding this book.

Step 2 – Share Your Story

In your caption, reflect on the significance of those shoes in your journey—your challenges, growth, and triumphs. Let the world see what these shoes represent in your life.

Step 3 – Spread the Inspiration

Post your photo and caption on Instagram, Facebook, X, TikTok, or LinkedIn. Use the hashtags below to connect with others and celebrate your unique shoe stories.
Tag @ChanelleColemanWesley so I can celebrate with you!

Step 4 – Pass the Baton

Think of a woman with an inspiring story. Tag her in your post, challenge her to read this chapter, and invite her to share a photo with her favorite shoes, this book, and her story.

I can't wait to read your stories and see those shoes, Sis. I'll be watching the tags and leaving comments.

Hashtags to Use
#SheSaidYesToHerselfUnapologetically
#IAmReleasingWhatNoLongerAligns
#RedDesignerShoeChallenge

Chapter Fifteen

Beyond the Lines: Embracing a Life Without Limits

Hello Gorgeous....

Empowering Declaration:

Remember to color outside the lines.

It's been a minute, but I still vividly remember my elementary school days. I loved my teacher, Mrs. Grant, and one subject I had a love/hate relationship with was art. Every art assignment began with her standing in front of the class with a visual aid, demonstrating what the completed project or coloring sheet should look like. She'd provide instructions, and remind us, "Children, don't forget to color inside the lines."

As she handed out the materials, the class would work earnestly to earn her approval. She'd walk between the desks, inspecting our work. If she paused too long by a desk, it meant one of two things—she was either admiring the work or thought it needed improvement.

Coloring Inside the Lines:Lessons from Art Class

I loved art, but I hated the inspections that followed. Once assignments were completed, our names went on our papers or projects, and Mrs. Grant would display them for all to see. That's when the real scrutiny began, children offering brutally honest compliments or critiques. Unlike Mrs. Grant, who always kept her opinions to herself.

Then there was Montreal. He never stayed within the lines. Bold, daring strokes with no apologies. We criticized him and reminded him of the instructions, but he remained unfazed. His work always stood out from the pack and he proudly displayed it, blissfully unconcerned with the need to conform. I, on the other hand, craved approval. My stomach in knots with worry over what others thought. Meanwhile, Montreal? He was living to the beat of his own drum.

For years, I thought "Poor Montreal had missed the assignment."

The Mirror Moment

Looking back, I realized Montreal wasn't reckless at all.
He was showing us what freedom looks like while I was busy coloring someone else's idea of perfect.

It wasn't until I reflected on my life that I realized he had understood the assignment perfectly, while I had completely missed the mark. I measured my work against a flawed standard, chasing approval and my idea of perfection, a mere replica of my teacher's work. Montreal? He wasn't concerned with validation; he was too busy using the boldest strokes, the most daring colors, and coloring outside the lines.

The Ripple Effect: When Life Imitates Art

If life keeps handing you blank pages, don't waste them tracing someone else's outline. It's time to create your own masterpiece. That shift didn't happen overnight, but every bold step rewrote the limits I once believed were unshakable. Growth demands movement. At some point, you have to stop tracing lines and start drawing a life that's completely your own.

It's funny how life imitates art. For years, I lived inside the lines—avoiding risks, shrinking myself, and confining myself to a box of limitations. But life kept presenting circumstances that forced me to step beyond my comfort zones. What began timidly grew bold, confident, poised, and powerful. Now that I've embraced a life beyond limitations, I refuse to shrink myself to fit into any box.

And Sis, I want you to do the same. Living inside the lines may feel safe, but true growth begins when you dare to step beyond those boundaries. Stop letting glass ceilings shaped by your own perceived limits hold you back. Shatter them. Embrace the limitless possibilities that await

Celebrate Your Uniqueness
Here are practical tips to living a life outside the lines:

The 7 Bold Commandments for Living Outside the Lines

Thou Shalt Not Seek Validation
Be your own thermostat. Draw confidence from who God created you to be, not from external applause. Set the temperature and let others adjust.

Thou Shalt Not Live Inside the Box
You are more than what others define as possible. Your vision is bigger than the box they've tried to place you in. Step out—live beyond limits.

Thou Shalt Live Boldly Outside the Lines

Comfort is the enemy of growth. Get comfortable with being uncomfortable. Take risks that scare you. Speak up, live out loud, and step beyond every line drawn to limit you. Bold is the new black—take up space unapologetically.

Thou Shalt Learn from Setbacks

Setbacks are setups for something greater. Every failure is a stepping stone to your next breakthrough.

Thou Shalt Not Quit

Quitting is not an option. Your boldest self is waiting to emerge. God hasn't given up on you—so you can't give up on you!

Thou Shalt Empower Others

You may not be where you want to be yet, but you can inspire others right where you are. Encourage yourself and those around you. Lead by example, lift others into their power, and watch your community rise with you.

Thou Shalt Love Thyself

Sis, you are fearfully and wonderfully made—God's own poetry in motion, a masterpiece dripping with divine intention and favor. Look yourself in the mirror and speak life over the woman you see looking back at you. Loving yourself isn't optional, it's a mandate from Heaven. Fill your cup until it overflows and let the overflow bless the world. Love yourself so unapologetically, so boldly, that doubt chokes on the thought of touching you.

Self-Work Activity

◆

Live Outside the Lines Challenge

This week it's time to move different. For seven days straight, dare yourself to step outside of your comfort zone every single day. Don't overthink it—big or small, every bold step counts.

Start a conversation with someone new.
Try a food, hobby, or experience you've never touched before.
Speak up in the meeting where you'd normally stay quiet.
Take that risk you've been rehearsing in your head but were too afraid to voice.

Each day, pause and reflect on what you did, how it stretched you, and what it revealed about the powerhouse you really are. Notice the discomfort—it's proof that you're growing. Celebrate the courage. Applaud the tiny wins.

Every time you refuse to shrink, the woman you are becoming takes notice. Every stride is a declaration that you will not be boxed in, silenced, or hidden. Your growth is your calling, your movement is your ministry, and your boldness is the proof that God's hand is all over you.

So take the leap. Step outside the lines. And watch God meet you in every brave, beautiful step.

Chapter Sixteen

The Table

Hello Gorgeous....

Empowering Declaration:

God grant me the wisdom to remove myself from tables you would've flipped over.

This isn't just an affirmation—it's your declaration of self-worth. As young girls, we were spoon-fed fairytales that taught us that contentment, peace, and our happily ever after began when a man decided to love us.

Newsflash: Before the stars were hung and the oceans knew their borders, God chose you. Long before anyone had an opinion, Heaven already approved you.
If He chose you, Sis—why wouldn't you choose you too?

The Table of Legacy
It is our responsibility and our privilege to build and pass down wealth to the next generation. Scripture reminds us that "a good person leaves an inheritance for their children's children."
We are called to be intentional—creating streams of income,

building assets and setting systems in place so the ones coming behind us are provided for and positioned to go further than we ever could.

But let's be real—money isn't the only thing we pass down. Too often we pass down debt, trauma, and hand-me-down mindsets that choke the very legacy we're trying to build. We leave trust funds but keep the trust issues. Passing down money without dismantling toxic thinking is like pouring water into a cup with a hole in it—it won't hold.

Generational curses don't break themselves. If we don't confront the thinking that held our mothers and grandmothers hostage, our daughters will inherit the same chains—just dressed in designer clothes.

Pause and ask yourself: What are you really leaving behind—faith or fear, discipline or chaos, purpose or patterns that keep your family stuck?

Healing the Table You Inherited

Prayer: *Father, give me courage to confront the patterns I've inherited and wisdom to break every chain.*

I grew up hearing, "What goes on in Mama's house, stays in Mama's house." That cryptic curse became a hiding place for pain. A saying meant to protect a home was hijacked by predators.

For a time I repeated this same pattern of silence, until I learned to speak uncomfortable truths. Now I'm intentional about instilling a new mindset in my children so they don't pass silence to theirs.

Identify the "family rules" you absorbed—spoken or

unspoken. Pray and declare which ones stop with you. Remember: What doesn't show up in the wash is revealed in the rinse.

Where Power Sits
Prayer: *Father God, cover my table with Your peace and reveal who belongs in each seat.*

The strength of your table isn't measured by how pretty the place settings look, it's measured by the weight of God's presence and the prayers that hold it together. A table without prayer is just cozy furniture—cute but powerless.

Think about the friends who carried the paralyzed man to Jesus. They sweated in the heat of the day, straining under the weight of his body. They pushed through crowds, climbed a roof, ripped it open—just to get their friend to the only One who could heal him. That's the kind of covering every woman needs. Friends who don't just show up for brunch selfies, but who will sweat, labor, and tear through barriers to bring you before the throne of grace.

And don't miss this: you can have friends who bring plenty of earthly benefits—connections, laughter, opportunity—yet add no spiritual depth. If they can't carry you to Christ, they can only carry you so far. *Knowing Jesus and knowing how to access Him is the real flex.*

Ejecting Chairs: Remove Toxic Seats
Prayer: Father, open my eyes to see who truly belongs at my table. Give me the courage to remove every seat You haven't assigned and the wisdom to protect what You've entrusted to me.

Some people don't want relationship—they want access.

Access to the call on your life, your anointing, your favor. I've invited people to my table so we could all eat, and while I was serving plates they were studying mine—plotting, taking notes, trying to figure out how to shake my table to build their own.

But hear me, Sis: tipping my table will never fill your plate. What God has prepared for me can't be stolen, duplicated, or dismantled. My growth isn't limited by what's on your plate, and yours isn't fed by trying to empty mine.

Your table is sacred. Every seat matters. Conduct regular "table audits." Identify those who disrupt your peace or threaten your progress. Remove them. **Believe them when they show you who they are.**

Seasons, Shifts, and Sacred Tables
Life moves in seasons, and your table moves with it. Some seasons stretch you wide—making room to invite new people and grow your influence. Other seasons pull you inward for healing and reset. Don't fight the rhythm. Embrace every shift God allows.

And remember this: tables turn. If your table isn't positioned the way you need, don't sit in silence, turn it over. You have the power to pivot, shift, and reclaim your space.

Sometimes the boldest move is the one that makes the loudest noise. Never be afraid to flip a table over. This isn't about furniture, it's about asserting your worth. Cut ties with anything that undermines your purpose. Indecision is a decision, Sis—and sometimes the only way forward is to flip the table and start fresh.

Self-Work Activity

Show Your Table

These are the ones who pray when I can't stand. My table is built on prayer and purpose. These are the women who carry me.

Your Turn:

Post a photo of your tribe—the women who pray for you, uplift you, and help you carry the weight.

Write a caption celebrating how they strengthen your table.

Use the hashtags #TheTable #EmpowerHERBlueprint #StrongTablesPray and tag me @ChanelleColemanWesley so I can celebrate with you and cheer on your circle of strength.

Your Next Step

If this chapter stirred something in you, there's more waiting for you at The Table.

Join my EmpowerHER membership community for only $19.99/month to access the full expanded chapter, deep-dive workbook, and weekly prayer & goal-setting calls.

Email shesaidyestoherself@gmail.com or visit www.shesaidyestoherself.com

to start your journey and secure your seat at a table built on faith, purpose, and unstoppable growth.

Chapter Seventeen

Slaying Self-Sabotage: Take Your Own Foot Off of Your Own Neck

Hello Gorgeous.....

Scripture:

Joshua 10:22-25 reads:
Then said Joshua, "And it came to pass, when they brought out those kings unto Joshua, that Joshua called for all the men of Israel, and said unto the captains of the men of war which went with him, 'Come near, put your feet upon the necks of these kings.' And they came near, and put their feet upon the necks of them. And Joshua said unto them, 'Fear not, nor be dismayed, be strong and of good courage: for thus shall the Lord do to all your enemies against whom ye fight.

In ancient times, placing your foot on the neck of a defeated enemy symbolized dominion, strength, and power. It marked the victor's supremacy while rendering the enemy powerless and utterly defeated.

Joshua's act conveyed this imagery powerfully.

The scriptural references about making your enemies your footstool are a foreshadowing of Jesus Christ's victory over Satan. Soon, Satan, our greatest foe, will literally be under our feet.

But what happens when you realize the enemy you are fighting and losing countless battles to isn't external—it's within? *What if the problem is the person staring back at you in the mirror? What if your foot is on your own neck? This is self-sabotage.*

Sis, pause for a moment. Take a breath and look in the mirror. See that person staring back at you? That's the person you've been either helping or hindering. Self-sabotage isn't always loud—it often whispers, "You can't," "Not yet," "It's too late," or "Wait, the time isn't right."

Ask yourself: Where in my life am I standing in my own way? What victories have I delayed because of doubt?
Be honest, Sis. Naming it is the first step toward slaying it.

Here's the truth: God has equipped you to overcome these inner battles. Just like Joshua placed his foot firmly on the necks of his enemies, you too can claim authority over the habits, thoughts, and fears that have kept you stuck. Victory begins in your mind, your choices, and your daily actions.

Overcoming the Inner Critic: A Path to Progress
What is Self-Sabotage? Self-sabotage can be conscious or subconscious actions that one takes—or refuses to take—that block success, preventing us from

accomplishing our goals. These behaviors stop us from reaching attainable achievements. The enemy isn't always someone external, your enemy could be you.

Before we dive into strategies, take a moment to journal, reflect, or even speak aloud:

"I am done holding myself back. I will no longer let fear, doubt, or insecurity dictate my future. I choose progress over perfection, action over hesitation, and faith over fear."

Seven Signs of Self-Sabotage
1. **Perfectionism:** Waiting for everything to be "just right" can keep you stuck.
2. **Procrastination:** Delaying important actions creates habits that sabotage your future.
3. **Failure to Communicate:** Not asking for help or expressing your needs can close doors.
4. **Negative Self-Talk:** Inner dialogue that magnifies self-doubt and insecurity.
5. **Self-Handicapping:** Making things harder for yourself through excuses or avoidance.
6. **Relationship Sabotage:** Pushing away people who could help you grow.
7. **Inability to Set Boundaries:** People-pleasing and lack of moderation prevent you from prioritizing what matters.

Sis, if any of this hits home, don't panic and don't you dare shrink back—you are not alone. The enemy loves to hide in plain sight, and sometimes the battle isn't "out there," it's the quiet war happening inside. Half the fight is realizing you have been standing in your own way. And when the light finally comes on, guilt will try to lock you in a prison of "should've, could've, would've."

But hear me: guilt is not your address.
Recognize the pattern, call it by name, and then refuse to stay there. Learn the lesson, break the cycle, and move with intention. This is your turning point. Get up, shake the dust, and step into the purpose that's been waiting on you all along.

Transparency Moment
I didn't learn to ride a bike until I was ten years old. Now Sis —don't judge me. I loved my red tricycle. I would ride it until my little legs got tired, like I owned the block. But eventually, I outgrew it, so my parents bought me a pink and white Big Wheel. I loved riding it and I thought I was Ms. Big Time, cruising the neighborhood. But soon, I outgrew that too.

Imagine my surprise when my parents gifted me a beautiful yellow and blue BMX bike for my seventh birthday. I still remember my father wheeling it into the living room. All my friends oohed and ahhed in approval, and at first glance, I loved it too. But as I walked closer, my excitement turned to dread when I noticed it was missing one thing, training wheels.

Fear crept in immediately. I thought to myself, I'm going to fall.
And I did. Hard.

My dad encouraged me to try again, holding on a little longer, but as soon as he let go, I fell again. Each fall felt worse than the last. "Don't worry, keep trying—you'll get it," my dad encouraged. But I didn't. I got back up, tried again, and fell even harder, scraping my hands and knees. "Come on, Chanelle, get back up and get on the bike, Luv," he coached. Eventually, I gave up. The bike became nothing more than a decoration in the corner of our basement.

That decision stuck until my 10th Christmas. Everyone got new bikes, and I hated the idea of getting back on a bike. That summer, I reluctantly tried again, not wanting to be left behind, but it was just as bad as I remembered. Fall. Get up. Fall again. Miserable, I finally parked my bike in the yard and watched everyone else ride.

Darnell Steps In

That's when my foster brother Darnell rolled up beside me. "What's wrong, Chanelle? Why aren't you riding?" he asked.

"I don't know how," I admitted.

"I'll help you," he said confidently.

He coached me like his life depended on it. I wobbled, fell, got back up, and tried again. I scraped my hands and knees, tears welling in the corners of my eyes. Frustration boiled over. "I'm not riding this stupid bike anymore," I said through clenched teeth.

Still, I climbed back on the bike—not because I wanted to keep trying, but because I was too far from home to walk it. My only goal was to get back home and park that bike.

Darnell trailed behind, shouting, "Chanelle!" I ignored him. "Chanelle!"

"What, Darnell?" I snapped, knowing he was trying to convince me to keep going. But I had had it.

"Chanelle, you're doing it!"

I looked down—and realized he was right.

And just like that, it happened. Without even noticing, I had finally figured it out.

Where Are You Standing in Your Own Way?

Sis, pause right here and get honest with yourself.

What opportunities have you already talked yourself out of?

What doors has fear convinced you were locked—while God was holding them wide open?

Think about every goal you've delayed, every step you didn't take because you thought you weren't ready. Those moments weren't failures; they were lessons preparing you for this very season.

What would your life look like if you walked as though every blessing you've been praying for was already yours?

Ask yourself: *Where am I standing in my own way? What patterns keep circling back to block my progress?*

Write it down. Speak it aloud. Lay it before God and let Him show you the next step.

Self-sabotage loses its grip the moment you drag it out of the shadows and confront it head-on. Your freedom starts with the courage to face the mirror and declare, "Not another day. I refuse to keep my own foot on my neck."

Self-Work Activity

◆

Self-Work Activity: Slay Your Self-Sabotage

Step 1: Reflect on Your Falls
Think about the moments you've "fallen"—the times you hesitated, gave up too soon, or held yourself back. Just like when I struggled to ride that bike, each fall is a lesson, not a failure. Ask yourself:

- Where have I been tripping myself up?
- What patterns keep showing up that hold me back?

Step 2: Identify Your Coaches
Who has been your "Darnell," encouraging and guiding you through your fears? Who are the people, mentors, or influences that push you to rise when you feel like giving up? Take note of them.

Step 3: Name the Enemy Within
Self-sabotage is often a voice inside whispering doubt, fear, and "you can't." Write down what your inner critic is saying. Give it a name, face it, and understand it. This is your first step to taking your power back.

Step 4: Journal Your Insights
Use your journal to answer these questions:

- Where am I standing in my own way?
- Which habits, thoughts, or fears keep repeating?
- How have past "falls" prepared me to rise stronger today?

Self-Work Activity

◆

Step 5: Take Action
Pick one small but meaningful step you've been avoiding. Take it this week. Whether it's starting a project, having a difficult conversation, or setting a boundary—do it. Your action is the proof that you're reclaiming control over your life.

Step 6: Declare Your Power
Close your journal and say this aloud:
"It's time for me to get out of my own way, take my foot off my neck, and today, relentlessly chase my purpose."

Chapter Eighteen

Slaying Self-Sabotage: The Enemy Within

Hello Gorgeous....

Scripture:

"Do you want to be made well?" Jesus asked the paralytic." John 5:6.

The Foot That's on Your Neck Might Be Your Own
The man was within inches of Infinite Power—Jesus, the Healer, Creator of the universe, God Almighty Himself—yet instead of saying a simple yes, he launched into a list of excuses: why he couldn't walk, why it wasn't his fault, why the timing wasn't right.

Can you see him, Sis? Standing in the very presence of the One who could change everything, but shrinking back with explanations instead of stepping forward to receive the miracle.

That's self-sabotage. And Jesus healed him anyway—despite his excuses.
He does the same for us. How many times have you stood in the space where Infinite Power was available, and instead of

receiving the blessing, you started listing reasons why it couldn't happen? In this season, God is requiring you to be excuse-less. Take your foot off your own neck.

We know the power, the opportunity, the blessing that's available—but we stop ourselves with fears, doubts, and delay.

New Levels, Familiar Devils

I wish I could tell you that once I learned to ride my bike I conquered this wily foe, but that wasn't the case. New levels presented new devils. Every time I elevated, she showed up in new clothing—but the motive was the same: to talk me out of where God was calling me.

For years, I let her win until I finally faced the truth: the woman standing in my way, blocking my blessing, was me.
Every time I refused to pedal forward, I handed the handlebars to fear. That pause, that second-guessing—that's the voice that keeps you from accessing the blessing with your name on it.

Identify Your Patterns

Think about it, Sis:

- How many opportunities have you talked yourself out of?
- What doors has fear convinced you were locked while God was holding them wide open?
- Every delayed dream, every missed step is a lesson, not a life sentence. You can't undo the past, but you can reclaim your future.

The enemy isn't always a stranger—it's the choice to let doubt win, the decision to park your bike on the sideline instead of pedaling forward.

Fear isn't your enemy; it's your wake-up call. Notice it. Nod at it. Pedal anyway.
And when you fall, remember: the fall doesn't define you. Getting back up does.

Mirror Moment
Grab your journal. Get honest.
· Where am I making excuses instead of stepping into my healing, my purpose, my calling?
· What habits or thought patterns keep circling back to block my progress?
· What victories have I delayed because I doubted God's timing—or my own ability?

Name the pattern. Call it by name. Self-sabotage loses its grip the moment you drag it into the light.

List Your Excuses
Write them down. Every reason, every "not yet," every "I can't." Then confront each one and identify the lie behind it. Lies lose power when you call them out.

Mantra / Declaration
Say this out loud until your own ears believe it:

"I refuse to let fear, doubt, or excuses hold the pen of my story.
Today I choose courage over comfort, faith over fear, and action over hesitation."

Empowerment Through Accountability: Overcoming Self-Sabotage

Now let's develop a real plan to counteract self-sabotage. Awareness is the first step, but action seals the victory.

1. **Identify Self-Sabotaging Behaviors** – Recognize and call out the patterns (perfectionism, procrastination, negative self-talk, relationship sabotage, boundary issues).
2. **Challenge Negative Thoughts** – Replace self-defeating dialogue with life-giving truth and scripture.
3. **Set Realistic Goals** – Break big goals into manageable steps and celebrate each victory.
4. **Develop Healthy Coping Mechanisms** – Use prayer, mindfulness, exercise, journaling, or trusted conversations to manage stress.
5. **Create Accountability** – Surround yourself with people who motivate and also hold you accountable.
6. **Seek Professional Help** – Therapy or counseling can break deep-rooted patterns.
7. **Cultivate Self-Compassion** – Embrace mistakes as part of growth. Remember: failure isn't falling—it's refusing to get back up.

Action Steps
· **Identify the behaviors.** Call them out.
· **Plan your next move.** Write an action plan and commit to at least one bold step this week.
· **Practice Mindfulness.** Stay present; journal to track triggers and progress.
· **Communicate.** Ask for help. Advocate for yourself.
· **Celebrate Small Wins.** Every forward pedal counts.

The Enemy Knows You

Sis, sometimes the enemy knows your strengths, your weaknesses, even your secrets—and sometimes she wears your face. She whispers lies in a voice that sounds like your own, pretending to protect you. But you don't have to let her win.

Today, look yourself in the mirror and declare:

"I see you, I own you, and I refuse to let you control my story. I take my foot off my own neck and step boldly into the purpose God prepared for me."

Every scrape, every hesitation, every delayed yes was shaping you for this moment.
The miracle isn't in the pool—it's in your movement.
Pedal forward and watch God meet you in motion.

Self-Work Activity

◆

Self-Work: Slay the Sabotage
Is self-sabotage keeping you from leveling up, expanding your business, building your brand, or becoming your best self? Take the quiz and find out.

1. Do you delay or avoid taking action on important tasks or goals?
2. Do you frequently engage in negative self-talk or criticize yourself?
3. Do you make excuses that prevent you from pursuing your dreams or making progress?
4. Are you setting unrealistic goals—or none at all—leading to disappointment?
5. Do you hold yourself back in relationships or opportunities because of fear of rejection or failure?
6. Do you dismiss compliments or positive feedback, focusing more on your perceived flaws?
7. Are you avoiding asking for help when you need it?
8. Have you set perfectionistic standards that discourage you when things don't go as planned?
9. Do you resist stepping outside your comfort zone or taking calculated risks?
10. Are you repeating negative patterns even when you know they're holding you back?

Self-Work Activity

If you answered "Yes" to 6 or more questions, it's time to break the cycle.

Email shesaidyestoherself@gmail.com to join the Slaying Self-Sabotage 7-Day Challenge and start your breakthrough today.

Remember: God has already equipped you to win—now it's time to move like you believe it.

Chapter Nineteen

Thou Shalt Invest In Thyself

Hello Gorgeous.....

Scripture:

"Do you want to be made well?" Jesus asked the paralytic." John 5:6.

The Moment That Changes Everything
Cardinal Rule #1 to implementing what you learned:
Self-Investment

Self-Investment: The Key to Unlocking Your Next Level
Sis, let me tell you something right now—this is your moment. Not next week, not when everything is "right", not after the world gives you permission. This is it. The opportunity to finally invest in yourself is sitting right in front of you, and it's waiting for your answer.

One of the hardest lessons I had to learn on my path to self-development and building my business was this simple truth: investing in yourself isn't optional—it's non-negotiable. The most worthwhile project you'll ever work on is YOU.

My Story: Hesitation and Breakthrough

There was a time when I thought investing in myself was risky, even dangerous. What if I failed? What if I succeeded and it didn't look like I thought it would? What if I wasted my money, energy, and time? Every opportunity that came across my radar made my heart race—I knew it was meant for me. But instead of stepping forward, I stayed stuck. I rehearsed every reason why I shouldn't take the leap. Fear had the microphone, and let me tell you, it was loud.

Then one day, I flipped the question. Instead of asking why I shouldn't, I asked: What could happen if I did? What doors could open? What growth could I experience? That one shift— just that one thought—changed everything. I bet on myself. And Sis, let me tell you: it paid off in ways I never imagined.

Step One: Believe in Your Worth

Investing in yourself starts with belief. The fear of failure, the anxiety of the unknown, the whispers of doubt—they're all normal. But growth doesn't happen in comfort. You can't rise until you let go of what's holding you back: limiting beliefs, past mistakes, self-doubt. Betting on yourself is an act of courage, faith, and sometimes a little bit of stubbornness.

Breaking Down Barriers to Self-Investment

It's easy to get stuck. Fear, lack of time, finances, comfort, and doubt can paralyze even the boldest of hearts. Let's break them down:

- **Fear of Failure:** Failure isn't never getting what you want —it's never trying. Ask: What's the worst that could happen? And the best?
- **Lack of Time:** Sis, even 15 minutes a day can move mountains. Prioritize YOU.
- **Financial Constraints:** Stop thinking of this as a luxury

- You invest in your car, your home, your health—why not the most valuable asset: YOU?
- **Comfort Zone:** Nothing grows there. Step out and stretch yourself.
- **Self-Doubt:** Surround yourself with believers, mentors, and coaches who see the greatness you sometimes can't see.

The ROI of Self-Investment
When you invest in yourself, the payoff is enormous:
- Confidence that radiates
- Skills that elevate you
- Health that sustains you
- Relationships that fulfill you
- Financial growth that rewards you

Not investing comes with a cost too:
- Stagnation
- Low self-esteem
- Missed opportunities
- Regret
- Feeling stuck while life passes by

The Power of a Guide
Even the greatest heroes didn't rise alone. Michael Jordan had Phil Jackson. Serena Williams had Richard Williams. Misty Copeland had Raven Wilkerson. You need a guide too—someone to push you, challenge you, and hold you accountable.

It's Time to Bet on You
You've absorbed strategies, insights, and tools. Now it's time to act. Whether you're ready for private coaching, a membership community, or sharing your story with the world, your next step requires courage and commitment.

Self-Work Activity

Your Next Bold Step:

1. Private Coaching: Let's Focus on You
- This is VIP, Sis—one-on-one, breaking down barriers, setting goals, and making them happen.

- Weekly sessions tailored to where you are and where you're going.

- Accountability, strategies, downloadable resources, discounted merchandise, personalized tools to help you crush it.
- Packages start at $299/month.

2. She Said Yes to Herself Membership: Your Tribe Awaits
- You need a squad that gets it—a community of women cheering you on, holding you accountable, and inspiring you to keep going.

- Monthly workshops to build confidence, grow vision, and fuel dreams.

- Exclusive perks: first look and discounted pricing on events, master classes, digital tools, merch, and more.
- $29.99/month.

3. Share Your Story: Be Part of Our Anthology
- Your voice matters. Inspire others and leave your mark.

- Professional editing, marketing, and opportunities to shine through interviews and events.

- Join a powerful network of women making their stories count.
- $399 one-time investment | Upgrade options available

Sis, What Are You Waiting For?
The life you've been dreaming about isn't going to show up on its own. You have to go after it like your name is on it—because it is. Don't wait for the "perfect" moment, because it may never come. You are the only one who can make the decision to prioritize yourself.

Take Action Now
Connect with me at shesaidyestoherself@gmail.com or visit www.shesaidyestoherself.com to take your next step.
The first 10 women to sign up receive exclusive access to an exclusive gift.

Sis, the greatest version of yourself is waiting for you. Commit to this journey. Bet on you. Break through fear, doubt, and hesitation.

Step boldly into your next level.
On the other side of pain is progress.
On the other side of defeat is victory.
On the other side of sadness is joy.
On the other side of brokenness is breakthrough.
Every obstacle is an opportunity. Every fear is a lesson. Every step forward is proof of your power. And Sis? I'll see you there, cheering you on every single step of the way.
So lace up your shoes—because mountains aren't going to climb themselves.
Are you ready to rise?
Let's do this. Together.

About the Author

Chanelle Coleman Wesley is a proud mom of six amazing children and "GiGi" to three beautiful grandchildren—her greatest joy and daily inspiration. A survivor, storyteller, and woman of unshakable faith, Chanelle lives every day as proof that God's grace can turn pain into purpose. Inspired by her late mother's unwavering faith and love for storytelling, she carries forward a legacy of courage, resilience, and devotion to God. Her journey from trauma to triumph fuels a passionate mission to help women break cycles, silence fear, and walk boldly in the life God designed for them.

Beyond home, Chanelle is an international speaker, bestselling author, playwright, and EmpowerHER Strategist. She is the founder of CeCi's Ink, a creative hub that amplifies the power of HER story through books, plays, coaching, and collaborative projects. She is also the visionary behind the She Said Yes to Herself Unapologetically platform and the editor-in-chief of Hustl' HER Magazine, where she equips women of faith to embrace purpose, build businesses and brands, and rise above limiting beliefs with practical strategies and faith-filled boldness.

Chanelle believes transformation begins with a mindset shift, a solid action plan, and accountability. Through her books, workshops, summits, and coaching, she empowers women to dream with their eyes wide open and take fearless steps toward their calling.

Let's stay connected!
Email: shesaidyestoherself@gmail.com
Website: www.shesaidyestoherself.com
Follow and tag Chanelle on social media using #EmpowerHERBlueprint and #SheSaidYesToHerself to share your own breakthroughs and join the movement.

Connect with Chanelle Coleman Wesley

Don't hesitate to reach out! Visit
www.shesaidyestoherself.com or email
shesaidyestoherself@gmail.com today.

Follow Chanelle on Social Media
Stay inspired and connected across platforms:

- Facebook – Personal: @ChanelleColemanWesley
- Facebook – She Said Yes to Herself Unapologetically:
  Follow Here
- Instagram: @chanelle_coleman_wesley
- LinkedIn: @ChanelleColemanWesley
- X (Twitter): @ChanelleCWesley
- TikTok: @ChanelleWesley

Invite Chanelle to Speak
Interested in having Chanelle speak at your next event?
Email shesaidyestoherself@gmail.com to book her today.

For More Inspiration and Resources

• Get the Books – Dive deeper into empowerment with
Chanelle's life-changing reads.
• Get the Workbooks – Apply the strategies and put the
principles into action.
• Join the Tribe – Connect with a faith-filled community of
women committed to growth and purpose.
• Watch the Unapologetically Her Podcast – Real
conversations, bold truths, and empowering stories to keep
you inspired.

Visit www.shesaidyestoherself.com to grab your resources,
join the Tribe, and start your next chapter of empowerment
today.

LE COLEMAN
TIONAL DEVOTIONAL EXPERIENCE

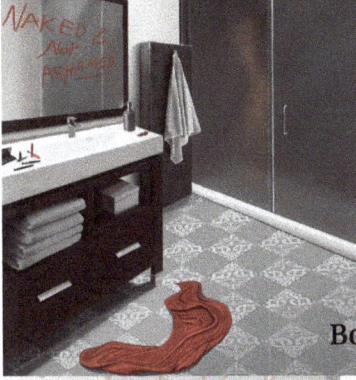

Books by Chanelle

Naked & Not Ashamed: The Transformational Devotional Experience

This powerful devotional invites you into a transparent sister-to-sister conversation where both writer and reader can expose their hearts without fear, judgment, or condemnation. It's a healing journey that strips away masks, charades, and pretense.

Through the familiar stories of women of faith—each marked by trial, triumph, failure, and redemption—you'll witness the resilience and transformative power of encountering Christ. Alongside these biblical accounts, Chanelle shares her own twists, turns, and lessons from her Christian walk.

But the most remarkable story is yours. Your breakthrough, healing, and transformation are found in the release of your story. This devotional challenges you to see the hand of God in your life and find the courage to share it.

Packed with thought-provoking journal prompts, engaging activities, and heartfelt prayers, Naked & Not Ashamed provides a three-sided mirror to help you unpack your narrative, embrace your journey, and unlock the power of your testimony.

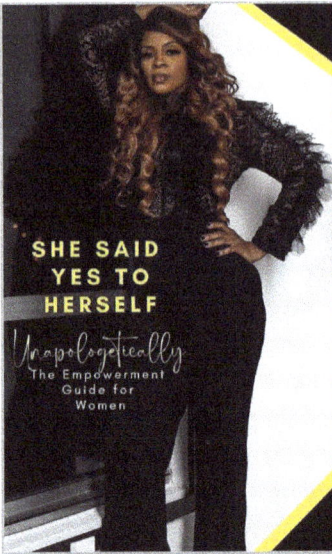

She Said Yes to Herself Unapologetically: The Empowerment Guide for Women serves as the anthem for women no longer content with serving themselves from empty cups. It urges us to stop shrinking to fit into spaces and places that no longer serve our growth. Instead, we reject the former versions of ourselves that sought validation from others.

We say yes because we remember the times we told ourselves no. We become unapologetic because we recall the moments we desperately sought permission from others. This book empowers women to exercise faith over fear, overcome limiting beliefs, and boldly walk in their divinely designed purpose. Through 21 principles, it shares valuable insights, truths, stories, affirmations, poems, and more.

Dedicated to women who yearn to embrace an empowered lifestyle, who crave change, who hunger for more, and who understand that the calling on their lives demands action. It's for those who recognize that to elevate themselves in every possible aspect, they must reach out and seize it with unwavering determination. Ladies, welcome to the revolution.

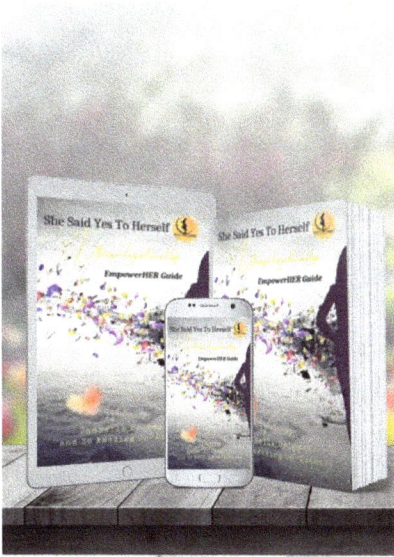

She Said Yes to Herself Unapologetically: EmpowerHER Guide

This dynamic anthology showcases the remarkable stories of 31 women of faith—change agents, bestselling authors, impactful speakers, professionals, and entrepreneurs—united by one mission: to pour purposefully, powerfully, and passionately into the lives of women everywhere.

Each narrative invites you to witness what happens when women dare to step beyond comfort zones and say yes to their God-given purpose. Inspired by She Said Yes to Herself Unapologetically: The Empowerment Guide for Women, these real-life testimonies reveal the profound impact of storytelling to ignite action, spark healing, and empower transformation.

Within these pages you'll find inspiration, encouragement, and practical guidance to help you navigate your own journey of growth, courage, and self-discovery. Whether you're facing challenges, pursuing big dreams, or embracing the fullness of your potential, the stories in this guide shine as a beacon of hope and empowerment for women everywhere.

Let's Stay Connected

Sis, this is only the beginning. I'd love to walk this journey of empowerment with you!

Visit www.shesaidyestoherself.com for resources, events, and updates.

Email me at shesaidyestoherself@gmail.com to share your story or invite me to speak.

Follow me on Facebook, Instagram, LinkedIn, TikTok, and X (@ChanelleColemanWesley) for daily inspiration and behind-the-scenes moments.

Your next chapter is waiting—and I can't wait to cheer you on as you write it.

www.ingramcontent.com/pod-product-compliance
Lightning Source LLC
Chambersburg PA
CBHW071123090426
42736CB00012B/1988